In the Name of Progress

'An Alternative Economic Model'

George Feneberg

DEDICATION

World Peace
Global Unification

CONTENTS

ACKNOWLEDGMENTS

Anyone making the world a better place.

1 CONSCIOUS REVOLUTION

Walter Rodney – "Revolution is the most dramatic appearance of a conscious people."

Take a moment to picture what the world would be at its best. Hopefully, most of you would end suffering and starvation, progress science and technology in an environmentally safe manner, and maintain high standards of freedom. If you agree, we share something in common. What stops society from achieving the best results for the species? To formulate a critically thought out opinion, this book investigates how societal structures enhance and limit us. In the term 'societal structures,' I include; religion, economy, education, and government.

Current societal structures have improved general living standards and progressed the species to what we are today; for that, they deserve supreme gratitude, but to assume our potential has been maximized seems naïve. History shows that societal structures have periodically re-shaped to represent the powers that were by creating the deterministic context in which masses live in. Using historical progress as an indicator, innovation within these societal structures fruits many advantages. However, today, mass production produces cities of garbage, threatening the natural environment, on which we rely to survive. Greed combined with scarce resource creates third world countries and limits people's ability to merely survive day to day making us a species that systematically kills our own in the name of something other than survival.

When we investigate who receives the lion's share of benefits from these structures, we notice that few people benefit in comparison with population numbers. A simple google search will land countless media reports on the dramatic differences in wealth distribution. That is not to say that wealth is a bad thing, not at all, instead, what you will find is that this book does not side with equal wealth distribution. Instead, the book introduces a new system for money supply that would replace the fractional reserve banking system to enhance progress. In this context, progress will be defined as; the means for securing the most beneficial future outcome for the most prolonged and most accommodating survival of the human species.

Our current economic system is one where money dictates survival and desires alike, which has allowed money to grow beyond a tool of barter. Money has become a tool of mind and body control, which no longer serves us, but rather, we serve it, or those who have money; and there is something wrong with this picture. We need to redefine money's ties to survival, or we will stay a race run by ego. I find it highly likely that this structural-economic update, among others, will create a free democratic society which will progress at faster rates than seen before. Automation is at a crucial point, that will wreak havoc within current societal structures without this adjustment. It is not our capabilities that hold us back, but our collective state of mind which has been contrived by current and historical societal structures. Why do our structures allow for the travesties we witness in countries deemed third in rank? What would it take to change?

In the big picture, we all stand to lose the same things; mother earth, our future, and freedom. If we cannot find a way to advance beyond this planet, our end may be sooner than could be. It is not a discussion of will it happen, but when will it happen? While astronomers look to the skies for asteroids, solar flares, or comets, geologists measure our risks here on earth from Yellowstone and the ring of fire's super volcanoes. When faced with great challenge, we, as a species, can work together to achieve the next step of civilization. We are, I believe, for the vast majority born internally good-natured, but easily influenced, by material possessions, traditions, symbols, and most of all, money, to become selfish. Those who are not good-natured, are genetic anomalies and detectable. Within each one of us, exists a faint voice, wondering why we look the other way… isn't there a better way? That voice that drives heinous violent crime offenders like Edmund Kemper to confess the murder of his mother. Even though violent extremities occur in people such as himself, we see the great in ourselves from Socrates to Martin Luther King and Susan B. Anthony. Yet, even with countless great minds who push us forward, our historically set societal structures hold us back. Much like me in my own life, we as a race are obstacles in our own progress toward a more forgiving future.

Current societal structures create a contrived paradigm for us, and populations become complacent due to the basic comforts it provides for working classes. This, in turn, has built up a long-term acceptance of these standards. One that has passed down through many generations. When things become too boxed in, we tend to lose sight of beneficial alternatives. Every once in a while, it's healthy to go through change like spring cleaning. We see this throughout history with advents from spirituality, paganism, monotheism, the Renaissance, to the Newtonian age and twenty-first century. There have always been moments that we collectively reflect upon ourselves and become better societies. We once burned innocent women over fairy tale beliefs that traditions fictionalized into society and enslaved our own kind to treat them as beasts of burden. Don't get me wrong, slavery still happens today, literally and metaphorically. In general, standards, are what have gotten better. I also wouldn't doubt there are religious fanatics out there still willing to burn people at stake.

The context in which we live, is very dynamic and should be treated as such. Imagine a person in their teens who looks at telephones in 1950, then at cell phones when they are in their 80's. A simple, but clear example, of how communication has gone out of context in a single generation. My argument is that current societal structures have become the old telephone from the fifties. The same societal structures have been adopted by most non-tribal nations around the world. Yet, these structures were not created with the populations of today's magnitude in mind. The U.S Census Bureau estimates 2.5 million people lived in the United States during 1776. Today with over 320 million the difference is staggering. Yet, representational structures remain the same. Global populations are even more prominent in comparison now to when the first monetary systems were used as early as 5000 BCE. For coinage around 700 BCE. Yet, very similar basic representational structures exist today. Back then, representation of the people was concentrated, which today is an especially important topic when it comes to government and the cultural diversity within nations.

An indicator of the catastrophic potential of centralized power within nations of such size is war. War is the ultimate evidence of the negative potential these societal structures have when concentrated groups of people with self-interest govern the masses through a highly centralized federal government. Thankfully, awareness is on the rise. Yet, manipulation of the masses is rampant non-the-less, when we have mostly the same fundamental societal structures in place that we had when we were witch hunters and shrine builders. Today, internet and technology have leapt us forward toward a more evolved self while disrupting the societal structures, human psychology, and the evolution of our minds. Access to answers has never been so easy. Google it! Technology and automation are the biggest advents we are faced with today, and I, for one, am a supporter of full automation. Bear with me, because if you do not agree with this, I intend to convince you that it is for the best. Ultimately, the Kardashev Scale sets us as a .72 civilization. We still have a lot of progress ahead of us, but the current societal structures that got us here are now a hindrance to favorable progression.

Before you read further, think about any injustices you see in the system for yourself. Do you notice any? I encourage you to leave bias at the door. To think in probabilities not in black in white. Allow for uncertainty even if it is against your nature to do so. Don't be glued to ideas, instead accept uncertainty. Let ideas be malleable. No matter how the subject impacts you, treat it as an exercise with an open mind. Robert M. Hensel once said, "the mind is like a sponge, soaking up endless drops of knowledge." No matter what hardship you are under or have endured, use it as a launching pad to better yourself. Gratefully soak up every bit of experience and knowledge that appears.

A conscious revolution may be coming but relevant societal structures that represent our modern good nature are necessary if we are to take a utilitarian approach to progress. By investigating many aspects of modern life, this book introduces a model for society which should produce minimal universal suffering, drop crime, lower stress, improve global economies, create robust free markets, and lead the way for a new age of social awareness.

2   Philosophy, Psychology, and Behavior

Philip Zimbardo – "Human behavior is incredibly pliable, plastic."

2.1 You're Your Own Patient.

We all have within us, our own mind to study; therefore, we are all students of psychology, with daily social behaviors to reflect on. For those of us not lucky enough to develop photographic memories, we're limited to journalizing our human interactions. Reflection allows the mind to prosper, without it we would still be in caves. Albert Einstein once said, "doing the same thing over and over again and expecting different results is insane."

Being aware of emotional states and desires is an important task. I tend to have a natural inclination to fight change and get distressed when something goes wrong. I sometimes build an attitude of harsh negativity when outcomes don't go my way, and I sometimes lash out in a way that is not productive. Only after the heat of the moment passes will I reflect on my actions and wish things went differently. In today's fast pace life style, many of us hardly have time to analyze our own behaviors; and who can blame us… with so much going on; forty-plus hour work week lifestyles, bills, taxes, and health problems. Self-reflections have become a luxury mostly available to those who have financial freedom, or those who do not work 40 plus hour weeks, and often those who don't work live in self-loathing for not having what the next person has, which can lead to psychiatrist billing you hours, that can, not will, be a slippery slope which can lead to permanent pharmaceutical drug addictions. Ultimately, it is our individual responsibilities to evolve and grow our own minds.

When I studied acting in my early twenties, we were given assignments to study the public's behavior and observe social ticks. Mostly, you notice uniqueness in older generations, because younger ones are often glued to cell phones. People are mostly the same with their general physical behavior these days… staring at their screens. Talk about an evolutionary path to a society of hunchbacks; on the other hand, it's shrewish behavior, good call Darwin. For this reason, I gave up on carrying my cell. I enjoy life disconnected from the network, even though I still often splurge with countless hours watching screens. This growing disconnect with nature is something we should re-consider. What would a world look like with our race proactively aiding biodiversity to enhance nature's flourish?

A problem with modern society is the easy access to distractions, but more so people's lack of self-discipline with them, myself included. Entertainment such as social media has greatly changed the way we self-reflect. With endless media sources to keep us informed and entertained, people hardly improve upon themselves. Instead, we spend our time watching funny videos and posting the best images of ourselves in attempt to create superficial online personas, when the truth cannot be displayed in pictures, it is internal. It is something you only get by spending genuine time with an individual. Time that allows us to drop built-up walls of mistrust against the world. A factor created by the self-serving societal structures we live in.

Google defines psychology as the scientific study of the mind and its functions, especially those affecting behavior in a given context. Our societal structures represent a large portion of the context of today's reality; therefore, have a large influence on our psychology. Only by examining ourselves daily to improve on our behaviors, can we truly discover our potential. Societal structures need to adjust periodically in order for individuals to change given how our psychology is influenced by them.

2.2 FREEWILL

I want to emphasize that all of these are thought experiments and do not represent any certain beliefs in my mind. Having said that, we all have within us the inevitability of death. If we are destined to die and there is only one possible outcome that can only be analyzed from a future perspective, it suggests that freewill is not free after all. For example, if 1 represents existing and 0 non-existing and we go from 0 to 1 then back to 0, that is evidence that we are pre-destined for death. Since time is linear in our dimensional state, only one possibility exists for each one of us to experience death. The thing is, we do not know the end result until we have reached it. Free will simply represents the choices of different actions we can take within the physical parameters specific to the time spent in the period 1. Logic indicates that if life is continuous, that it would follow the sequence 0-1-0-1-0-1-0 and so forth in a rotational pattern which correlates with physical reincarnation or simply is the representation of re-creation then death. This suggests we, our direct ancestors, and our children are all a single organism from a broad perspective.

Actions may likely have no impact on the persons time of death, as we all know that life is not fully controllable. In fact, life seems considerably uncontrollable; it takes unexpected turns which can be argued to be the major turning points that will ultimately lead you to your destined death. However, some believe they can manipulate and control their time of death. This can always be explained from the destined death perspective by the mere saying that it is an unexpected turn that will always lead to death. Even in the case of suicide, often it is an unexpected event or sequence of events that pushes an individual to commit it.

The discussion becomes not whether life is destined, because we know that it is indeed pre-determined at a fundamental level, but are our daily actions pre-destined as well? Hard-nosed logic would dictate that if death is predestined, why is the rest not also so? We should ask ourselves, can we program something with a final destined ending that is unaware of that ending? We see it in video games, every day. These virtual avatars have a predestined time of expiration and likely have no awareness of anything at all or at least from our perspectives, but also, they have not been programmed for such.

Though, in games like the sims, the avatars are programmed to automate themselves. We are third parties controlling their actions within their reality, as if giving them temporary 'souls'. This leads to the question of whether our reality is truly a genuine existence or a virtual creation, which many have come to ponder. Are we merely avatars for an external entity or 'soul' to control like the external force that drives the actions of our video game avatars today? Does there exist a 'real world,' like earth is the 'real world' of the avatars in our video games, and Hollywood's 'the Matrix' speculated in their savior story?

It could be that we are merely displaying our own 'soul-entities' natures in creating video games in our reality to play. That could suggest that even the 'real world' outside of ours itself could be another virtual reality created by yet another society of beings. It could also mean that they slow their own perception of time down in human awareness. The original 'real world' entities could have achieved approximate immortality this way unless they are naturally immortal. If they have discovered how to slow their perception of time let's say fourteen-billionth slower than in their 'real world', they could experience countless lives within our world within a single lifetime in theirs. Boredom and monotony is fixed by way of birth and death, the 'soul' or external entity in control of us gets to jump from one life to another and experience different things thus collecting a near infinite number of experiences.

In this hypothetical virtual reality view, we could assume that we do have freewill within the parameters of life to influence the outcome of our death. Like in video games, how the avatar may for sure die, but we are unaware of where or how at first. This would also suggest that we are merely avatars for an external entity or 'soul.' If this were the case than we do not have freewill, but rather it is the free will of these 'souls' or real entities that drive us. Hence, even in this possibility, it would be a point against our own free will. A problem for me is that a non-simulation world could be described as a simulation because a simulation is merely an attempt at re-creating a similar world to that in which it exists.

If life is destined to the very detail, as in, no such influence on our deaths whatsoever, that would suggest a pure viewer of our race, like a reality television show. Then free will is merely an illusion, and, in both cases, an external entity type creator is likely. In this case, we are merely scripted code that have been programmed with feelings and desires but whoever is viewing us takes pleasure in the act of watching, and to them, us trying to figure out what this all means may be humorous or intentional. This hypothetical view suggests there are multiple of these entities and possibly many of these sorts of realities.

Like Elon musk has stated, we will reach a point that we can create a virtual world that replicates our reality exactly. This will bring us one step closer to true immortality because it will get us closer to slowing our own perceptions of time down within these states. We could experience countless virtual lives within one normal human life. This may be the closest we can get to true immortality, as one day we know our physical world to end, but also this is the only way to achieve near perfect free will. If one can create a fake world to experience countless virtual lives, we could call ourselves near god like. We could solve all our problems by living different lives in virtual worlds like ours by making our mistakes there. So, is that what we are for some other world? Is that outside world also in danger of ending and thus we likely should understand how to survive natural dangers? Again, these are merely thought experiments, and completely hypothetical.

Much of life seems to come down to free will and how free it is. First off, we know there is no absolute free will; we cannot turn ourselves into hawks and fly away on a moment's notice. We are confined to certain natural laws, and for us to define free will, we should also identify a spectrum of possibilities that could encompass 'free-will' in period 1. Free will seems probable to be merely a human formed concept determining nothing. The fact that we cannot determine the future to 100 percent certainty creates the illusion of free-will. We can only analyze things of the past, and we cannot stop 'space inflation' as far as we know, but also, I'm no expert in astrophysics. Yet, if you try and stop doing everything, life around you will not stop for you.

If free will does exist, it is not absolute. There are many aspects of determinism that cannot be debated as per the evidence that exists. Though from my perspective the only fact and plain evidence needed to realize that something such as free will does not exist is the linear nature of age progression and what we term 'time,' but as I will always hold true taking faith on any uncertainty is irrational, so to me that stays unknown.

The fact that we are put in an externally driven environment, we do not know what will happen tomorrow, and all we have to go on is the past, it seems that true free will would only exist in a world where the no such thing as death would exist. We could form ourselves and our environments into anything with mere thought. Like having complete control of a dream sequence. That would be 'free-will' to me. Otherwise, we know we are bound by the laws of physics. Free will seems to go out the door with that concept. The debate seems so irrational that to spend time on it seems only the outcome of a world where free will does not exist. Why? Because even at the face of a linear timeline and the laws of physics, some will still believe it exists. If they had free-will they would surely come to that understanding, but then again, uncertainties can never be certain, so I take no stance on such topics.

However, if free will is genuine, this world is more likely created by a force or energy source that likely has no conscious, and we are merely 'lucky' to exist. In all outcomes, we should preserve this ever so improbable event, that is our existence, and preserve nature's biodiversity to co-exist with our needs as practical for efficient survival. If we can influence the environment and our world shapes itself from our collective beliefs, our results reflect the nature of our collective morality; for that reason, it is crucial for us to persistently re-mold societal structures. In the event that we have genuine freewill, we should also take the probabilities of other intelligent life forms seriously. Since the universe is so vast, it is highly probable that space has abundant intelligent life, given 'free-will'. It would also seem likely that we would not be the first to develop intelligence given that the universe may have existed forever behind us, which brings us to the equally important question; is the universe infinite or finite?

2.3 INFINITE UNIVERSE?

Being an infinite universe, we take the assumption that every possibility is, has been, or will be a reality, but also is all being so at the same time. And for the universe to be infinite nothing anyone can come up with can be denied. Though, we have to accept that there is only one reality and truth to the environment relevant to us. This suggests that nothing is impossible, which is an interesting take on the universe if you are a writer of fiction, because that means every single story ever told is, has been, or will be a reality. So, is fiction an accurate concept?

There is no time from an outside perspective, only motion and mass within an infinite space. I am not an experimental physicist, so I cannot develop solid evidence for such concepts, but merely present a layman's hypothesis. It seems to depend on whether we are indeed a natural occurrence by inanimate-non-conscious things such as dark matter and gravity or are we a virtual type world created from an external world of intelligent beings. It seems that a lot of philosophical concepts hinge on this being true or not. For example, the existence of a creator and the afterlife. I also do not take a certain stance on such a topic. I merely ponder the idea, being that I take an agnostic view on this subject.

2.4 CREATOR

Because life has physical parameters, it provides a system of functionality. Therefore, should have a source. For something to exist without a source, it seems no parameters would exist like an order-less plane mix of substances or none at all. One could describe it as chaos. From this chaos, a force or condition molds substance into shapes, which suggests nothing is real, but merely a thought or information external to this source. This ultimate force or set of conditions that mold physical reality is what objectively is a creator. It may not be aware. It would have existed before all planets even if this is a virtual world. Because 'creator' is merely a term we invented to describe a person or thing that brings something into existence, we can see that 'god' or the force that brought us into existence is more of a force or condition like gravity. This force may not have consciously created us but rather been a function that accidentally put us here. By looking for a meaning set by a creator, we may be sending ourselves on a wild goose chase with no significant meaning to discover.

Creator of life could also be argued to be the combination of sun light and chemicals on earth. This way of explaining things is simply a practical way of looking at how the natural world comes about. If this is indeed a simulation than reality may have dramatically different parameters. An entity creator of existence is likely not a relevant concept. Especially, if existence has always been. Most likely it would be nothing more than a thought or idea. To think about god in a form of a living entity that created humanity is improbable. Science explains created the human and life on earth was indeed the sun and the atmospheric conditions of earth for which we have gravity to thank. If you want to get literal about it, those are 'creators.'

2.5 NATURE VERSUS NURTURE

Both biological and hereditary predispositions have influences on people's physical appearances, fears, and behaviors, but emotionally charged events are what create the belief systems in a person's mind that mainly guides behavior. I notice this in myself often. My journey through life has taken me from a German birth to Brazil, at the age of three, to the United States at the age of eight, and Canada at the age of fourteen. In Brazil, as a youth our house was invaded by armed robbers, and that event has molded so much of my life including how I sleep. I jump out of bed at any strange noise ready for a fight and always lock the door.

When I was twenty-three, I re-located for a second time to Vancouver from Brazil and had nothing but one month's rent and a car. My car, which I lived in, had a problem and I took it to a friend's suggested mechanic who charged me eight hundred dollars, which was half my rent money. Months later, I found out that it was a simple fifty-dollar fix. That event for ever painted a negative image of mechanics in my mind, which later affected my behavior toward mechanics and heightened my awareness of 'cheap talk.'

Another simple example was my first serious girlfriend of which I thought I was deeply in love. She ended up cheating on me with a guy I knew and kept doing so for three months while we were together. When she told me, it felt like a ton of bricks landed on my chest. For two weeks, I sat depressed in my room, contemplating relationships. For many years afterword's, I took out my frustrations on girls. I could only maintain flings and relationships where I intentionally broke hearts without care. It created a belief system within me. These charged moments have molded me among others from my life, as I'm sure yours have as well. My relationships still suffer from the romantic trauma my first girlfriend put me through. People will try to advise you to forget the past but you likely should accept the past to forget it. The present can only be enjoyed when the past has been accepted.

Part of me wants to set a high probability that partial hereditary memories get transferred from ancestors down to us as experiences affect their genetics and gets passed down, but I'm not sure how to go about proving that. Taking logic into consideration, all of our parent's experiences prior to conceiving us get passed down by genetics, which would suggest many aspects of personality and character are determined through genetics. This is clear when it comes to physical features and the evidence is beyond a doubt. The deeper question, is whether it also affects our natural fears or desires. I for one am deathly afraid of being out in deep water. I never really understood why, then one day, my father told me that he and my grandfather were the same way. I find it likely that this stems from an ancestor's previous bad experiences with the ocean and travel. My close friend always got very nauseous when he saw decapitations in a film. I mean, we all do, but it had a profound impact on him even knowing that it was acted in a fiction film. We always joked that it likely should've been one of his ancestors who almost got his head chopped off or watched someone get decapitated. Another indication that we and our ancestors are one living organism. This is further indicated by those experiences when you meet people that you instantly get along with or do not get along with.

A possibility exists that your past ancestors have met, or you may share some gene specifications. I want to reiterate the speculative nature of such a hypothesis. Even though experiences get passed down, I find it likely that much can be re-molded during a person's life; therefore, I don't regard genetics as a leading indicator of human behavior. Especially, since the genes of two people is diluted to form a new person. Unfortunately, that is the only speculative evidence I have on such a topic. Ancient triggers exist in us, such as when people fasting can't sleep because the brain is telling them to search out food. These are examples of the experience embedment that occurs through evolution. We cannot avoid things that have formed into our hereditary genetics, but we can notice them and try to make a difference.

Nurture seems to have a more significant impact in how I behave than nature, but again, more than anything else are emotionally charged-events that mold underlying belief systems that ultimately have a large influence on my behavior. What this seems to suggest is that societal structures as outlined in my book are a determinant of 'nurture.' Societal structures influence all moments in our lives which form our belief systems and eventually influence our behaviors. Societal structures not only regulate and set forth all the rules for us to follow, they enforce them with medieval punishment in most places around the world. It is our desires and ambitions that drive us, but who dictates what is a good desire and ambition? Our societal structures tell us everything; how to behave, how to dress, what jobs are the best, and what we should do for fun. The systems we have in place pre-date rational thought and represent a self-centered view on things based on old servitude. This in turn creates self-centered humans who care little for their fellow neighbors, even though we share this planet and will suffer the same fate given a large catastrophe. The biggest moments that determine individual's behaviors are their interactions and experiences with other people, major failures and downfalls, or victories; all of which are well determined and highly influenced by our societal structures.

2.6 SUBCONSCIOUS

Our brains record everything around us… every single bit of stimuli. I define subconscious in this book as; the parts of your brain other than your prefrontal cortex. We seem to have limited control over our subconscious cognition or so we have grown to think. In everyday living, the prefrontal cortex is the most active part of our brains and represents a large portion of our brains, likely due to the increased of bureaucratic rule. We need the prefrontal cortex to learn rules, and societal structures have created an inefficient amount of them. Societies are covered with bureaucracy, when there need only exist one underlying principle, 'treat others and their belongings the way you want others to treat you and your belongings.' Do our societal structures represent this rule?

Even when we look across the street, our minds automatically calculate time, distance, and speed within a fraction of a second to know whether it is safe to cross or not. We all have an active mind… how would you feel if all your thoughts were broadcast publicly without interruption? Would you feel comfortable with everything that people might find? Do you pay attention to what is going on deep within the confines of the rest of your mind? Do you ever get thoughts that make you wonder where they came from, like intuition to make a decision? Decisions that may not include stakes but presents itself like intuition… like taking one street instead of another when walking or driving your car. Our subconscious, is never-endingly at work connecting dots to feed us intuitions that our prefrontal cortex may not pick up on.

Sleep is our subconscious realm, so paying attention to dreams and following your intuition about them without pre-frontal cortex interruption is one way to use your subconscious mind. Meditation works wonders as well. When Meditation practitioners tell you to stop thinking, they mean the pre-frontal cortex, because when you can shut off that part of your brain, you can become more aware of your subconscious. Studies show that patients with damage to their prefrontal cortex show insensitivity to future consequences of their actions. (Antoine Bechara, 2002) This suggest that when monks go into a meditative trance, they train their brains to shut off their prefrontal cortex. By doing so they are more care free about life and surpass the fear of death or harm.

Once societal structures establish rules that form within our prefrontal cortex through multiple generations, they likely embed into the evolutionary process and may take generations to undo. The longer we evolve this way, the further we get from our highest collective potential. Taking less consideration to the development of our subconscious likely had an influence on our decreased brain sizes in the last 10,000 thousand years; but that is my own idea. In the last hundred it has begun a reverse writes Scientific America. (Hawks, n.d.) To enhance this rebound, we should consider focused attention to our subconscious development.

Many who influenced the gradual development of societal structures were often in the ruling party of radical ideologies with self-interest at heart when developing much of the society we see today. Many historical figures believed in fictitious deities and cared only for their continued reign over others, and at the time, who was to blame an aware person to best look out for themselves? Ancient leaders more often than not didn't have the common good of everyone at heart when molding these structures. Yet, we still follow similar paradigms today, even though morality and the study of it are available to all in the world. If we continue to live with ancient societal structures, we will always be divided by them. Only with the re-development of current societal structures, to the relevancies of the twenty first century, can we move forward into a more productive and peaceful society.

We seem to have limited capacity to the amount of instantaneous information we can hold. This could be a self-imposed evolutionary trait we developed since the advent of writing. There is an old idea that the knowledge of the universe is all around us, and we merely have to listen for answers to appear. What this seems to me is misunderstandings of the power of the subconscious, which if we have stored a lot of specialized information of a subject, will automatically work for us without our direct awareness. Dedicated individuals who have exposed themselves to much specialized knowledge will feel like the ideas simply appear. Well if you put the right amount of information into the subconscious it will automatically work things out for you. This can be accelerated by belief-acceptance and habitual use of this concept. By going to sleep thinking of any issues that need resolution, you can further proactively guide your subconscious with positive suggestions. What we feed are brains before sleep becomes very important. Without specialized knowledge of our physical plain or whatever relative requirements for our ideas, our minds can merely write science fiction and conjure ideas of technologies not invented.

2.7 Final Words On Philosophy, Psychology, and Behavior

2.7.1 Double Slit Experiment

Math and physics are only human expressions of the things we can see and touch. Not an expert at all, but I have heard of the double slit experiment. I'm probably completely wrong, but us perceiving matter at a quantum level could merely be a phenomenon in how we perceive it and not it changing forms or behaving differently; meaning that nothing actually changes in the behavior of the particles. Instead, what changes is our perception of the end results, given we have expectations from it, kind of like, how the mind fills in colors in a black and white picture if you have seen the colored one right before it. This suggests the change occurs inside of us not the particles, and for whatever reason we only observe the result as our minds are made to and not as it is. I'm definitely no expert in that subject matter, but it's sure fun to think about.

2.7.2   Money's Power Over Psychology

Think for a moment about this… what do you notice? Do you think money influences psychology? True, there are those who give up the use of modern money to live in temples or out in the wilderness, but in modern societies money definitely seems to affect psychology. What I notice is that general people walk in the rich's footsteps and try to mirror them in every knockoff way. I have witnessed bizarre acts just to impress a person born into wealth. Money has become the physical representation of mind control, because it allows freedom from the stress of survival.

Today, money influences politics to an incredible extent. Will you deny this? Regardless of whether there is legislation setting low limits to political contributions, we cannot easily prove that 'special' contributions are not made voluntarily. This is a large problem dealing with very centralized federal governments who are responsible for the masses. Looking at recent American and Canadian political leaders, we see a clear pattern emerge. They are often of wealthy lineage with previous political ties.

The power money has over the psychology allows for rich people to attract common voters in the election process by using their looks and economic influence like they used to use alcohol. The representation is so obscured that very few people genuinely know these leaders personally, and likely the only people that know them, are only there for financial and social benefits. The general voter is meant to accept a leader they never sit down and have a meal with. Instead, they are presented with a personality whom might as well be a cartoon character that has been styled by a group of publicists that study general mass psychology to gauge your best response. Do not fall for this! Seems like pure manipulation.

The influence money has over the mind is so strong that it has led to devoted schools of thought, and countless books about how to get over it. We see single individuals growing their wealth beyond what any rational person could ever spend in a single lifetime with the most luxurious of lifestyles. The influence money has over psychology allows the rich to buy people like commodities. These adopted human beings are not put to labor but are mentally conditioned and stripped of their historical identities; something that can never be fully restored. Has the miracle of life devalued so far for family relations to mean nothing anymore? Will luxuries and empty euphoria be enough to keep an inherit curiosity for identity? The reason people can do this is because the very nations where they made their fortunes have indirectly and sometimes directly created the misery those very kids are in. If their adopters truly desire the best for humanity as their actions might intend, they likely should consider that the problem is fundamentally in modern societal structures.

Money can turn a good person into an addict. It is a sort of drug because of links to survival and its accumulating quality. When there is no end to the amount a person can accumulate, they will lead a life resembling that of a drug addict always trying to reach that next target. This is the type of influence over that mind that makes people participate and run schemes like Enron or any other major financial Ponzi scheme out there. The kind of influence that makes once innocent beautiful children turn into people who legally steal their employee's life pension. The kind of influence that creates elite restaurant or hangouts that exclude anyone that isn't above a certain wealth threshold. It creates social oligopolies dictating our social order. It influences people to create arrogant traditions that work against survival of the human race. Humanity is meant to evolve continually into something that we cannot imagine at this point, because the current fractional reserve banking system for money supply holds us back.

Realizing the influence money has over psychology likely should be understood to not succumb to its allure of guiding control over us. Rather, we should redefine it and not let it, or those who have it, define us. Money, or lack of it, should not dictate who we socialize with, or where we educate children. Money allows for a false sense of superiority that fosters separation. I say false, because we are all 1's and eventually 0's in a linear life cycle with only birth as a means of continuation. So, why is it that people are so influenced by money?

Like magic, it controls people literally. It will make a warrior dress in uniform with a bow tie and serve drinks. It will make mothers have orgies and more. It will make people jump off a bridge. It will drive people to sell their children to the rich. It will make men kill. Make them Massacre. Make them rape. Make them rob. And why? Over what? Really the truth is, more often than not, it is necessity of survival. Circumstances are created over money. Things go wrong. We must separate money and survival. They cannot be fully combined. This requires a needs-based money supply system as outline later in the book, that will cover basic necessities for the team.

2.7.3 Competitive Spirit.

Current societal structures push us toward a competitive mental state. Education ranks us by test score from the very beginning. Kids play board games, video games, and sports games created by our economic systems for profit, and our politicians compete based on popularity in government. Everything in the world includes the best of, and everyone starts off as a beginner. Organized sports have people compete to feel superior than the rest. Like a pyramid, with the winners at the top, almost everything falls into this pinnacle structure.

This ingrained competitive mental state traces back for centuries and may be impossible to completely get rid of, nor should we try. Competitiveness is a good quality given it doesn't lead to mistreatment of others. We should not let our competitive spirits get to the point where we put others down. Life is the ultimate team game for survival, and we should encourage one another because whether we like it or not, we're all on this team. Success is about progress and getting the best quality results, not feeling superior. I for one am a very competitive person, and I believe competition is essential to survival in the universe. But friendly competition is better than hostile. Competition serves to benefit the race not set us back. What is competitive spirit worth if it leads to arrogance in winners and depression in losers?

Psychology today's, Lisa Firestone, writes about how competitive thoughts are usually exaggerated, but claims it is healthy and I agree. (Firestone, 2013) What is healthy competition, and how is it, in the corporate world, that moral employees are to compete with people willing to bend rules and socially engineer situations to climb their way to the top? These corporate structures create animosity within organizations of people who have to work together, which demonstrates how societal structures encourage such counter-productive behavior from participants. That is why psychopaths have been suggested to move up quickly in business and politics. Books like 'The Wisdom of Psychopaths' and 'The Prince' have been written about it.

Today, success and the pure competitive spirit mixed with the long-ingrained need to feel superior leads society down a path of self-destruction. Even if people are not biologically unempathetic, many good people are coerced into immoral behaviors and actions in the market place due to competition, which is evidence of how people are not sovereign in their decision making because their actions are guided by the societal structures. Examples of this would be lawyers who have high moral values but end up working a law firm with lower morals in the name of money. In business, competition is good for innovation and healthy prices for consumers, but only in the short-term perspective and in the context of convenience. Being competitive is beneficial to both parties; the losing side gets to improve by competing with someone more skilled, and the winner improves their game by giving away their tactics, eventually forcing their repertoire to grow. For the best benefits to society, it follows that we should consider increasing friendly competition in our society and implementing this concept into our societal structures.

2.7.3.1 *Superiority*

The desire for superiority shows itself in public situations and especially in mixed gender group situations, where we see that instinctual behavior that people have. When two friends pursue the same girl, or simply want to impress a common colleague. Loyalties can be tossed aside rapidly. Even at a young age, I've seen rich youths make friends with less fortunate ones in order to feel superior to them. However, the sword can have a double edge, when the other friend may only be using the rich friend in turn to gain social status. What is friendship at that point? Yet, after spending genuine time together, they may realize they have things in common, as we all do, and develop a lasting bond.

In group situations, friends can quickly change in order to preserve his or her image with other friends of their social financial equivalent. We see it in high school teenagers most often as they have become more aware of societal structures and financial status. It doesn't happen often when kids are young. Children are much more curious and accepting of others. I notice the desire for superiority grow as we get older. This suggests a strong link between superiority and money, but also a disconnect between genuineness and money. Money is foreign to our natural system. Yet, money has come to define who we are, and sets us apart by measurable means. It has created many benefits but also grown out control.

The worst of it happens in the education system, when kids first understand financial status, which leads to kids from wealthy homes feeling superior to others regardless of whether they had anything to do with earning the money or not. Many times, it is not even their parents who earned the money, but their grandparents. Early wealth earned in families that is saved and passed down serves to create an unjustified sense of superiority. This feeling roots itself deep within our societal structures. From caste systems to social structures, we have always felt the need to place ourselves higher than our fellow brothers and sisters. The root causes being the separation of the species and the combination of our needs markets and luxuries markets.

We show this primitive behavior that roots itself in the 'only the strong survive' mentality of staying alive without modern technology. Like a lion is or gorilla is made king usually because of mere strength. In humanity, we have placed the people at the top who have nothing to do with surviving or earning but rather have been the luckiest. Donald Trump, George Bush, Justin Trudeau, all serve as great examples of the influence money has over the masses. All lineage leaders. Not saying they are bad, but that these are people who have never had to struggle for survival a day in their life. People who have been given falsified recognition based on image alone. Yet, the masses look up to them because, to the public, anyone who is in a better position in life likely should know better. These inheritors, that the populations elect as leaders likely have no perspective of the working-class individual. Yet, the majority of the population is working class. Representation today is far from near and the writing is on the wall.

The person with nothing will embrace death, while the person with everything will struggle with death. There is no point in superiority because there is no such thing with the existence of death. If one person thinks they are superior while the other person doesn't care suggests the person who needs to feel superior will always suffer because there is no such thing. They may always desire to feel this and will never achieve it from a person who does not believe in it.

We see the pure desire for superiority trait in people, who have become so naturally used to it from the environment, that not having it shocks them. Feeling superior to others is something that seems to root from vanity. We can become so invested in our own vanity that we put everyone down if they disagree on topics. A person born into money, is prone to never truly understanding the struggle for survival inherent to most of humanity. Leaders with such background are prime examples of how the masses can be manipulated by a candidate's wealth regardless of whether they earned it or not. Of course, that is not to say they cannot be wise, moral, and genuine people, but likely this character development would only manifest from some sort of dire struggle that most of them never go through. What this means is that there lies a greater responsibility in those parents to guide their children in the right direction.

2.7.3.2 *Positive or Negative Competition*

Positive competition allows for all parties involved to gain and is what we want for society. Being humble as a winner is crucial because someone younger, better, and healthier than you will come around someday whether it be in sports, video games, or science. The important thing, as Maya Angelou said, "people remember how you made them feel."

We see the benefits of competition all around us. History shows that the competition between Nikola Tesla and Thomas Edison likely lost the species progress, but also earned progress. The hindrance in our progression was JP Morgan's shutting Tesla's further experimentation with wireless energy. What it came down to was money back then, and what it seems to always come down to is, *money*. Nikola could have pursued his goal of harvesting energy in different ways, which stands as a prime example of how societal structures hindered progress. However, without societal structures, he would not have accomplished what he did, nor would he have done it without the competitive nature of his relationship with Thomas Edison. Yet, had Tesla had funding from the beginning of his career, it is quite possible that he could have discovered countless other technologies and fine-tuned things he was still working on. Now we'll never know.

Today, we see how competition can be manipulated to serve the few at the top. In business we have monopolies or oligopolies like OPEC. A small group of major oil producers who pretty much rig the oil markets. They in turn have a huge incentive to protect oil markets. These are not examples of healthy competition and represent evidence of an inefficient economic system.

2.7.3.3 *Vanity*

We portray ourselves to look the best we can to others. Reality is that we are not all born lucky enough to have symmetrical facial features and fast metabolisms that keep us in shape. Vanity runs girls lives in today's world. The market for cosmetics in the U.S alone is over fifty billion a year. So, how much does it affect our psychology and behavior? Well, it seems that it largely affects both, by possibly being a deciding factor in who we choose to mate with or pursue romantically.

Vanity product markets can define what users of their products do for large portions of their day, which becomes dedicated to vanity instead of self-progress. For example, my beloved girlfriend spends at least an hour on her vanity every day. When you think about that in a lifetime it adds up. In a lifetime she spends over one year of her life on vanity. You could argue the practicality of the use of the time, but in today's societal structure landscape, vanity will likely benefit a person's money-making abilities in the corporate world. Vanity serves to be influencer of other people. We use it to control how others look at us. In general, people are nice to those they are attracted too. So, is vanity a good thing? Sure, like all things moderation is key, but let's not combine vanity and hygiene, which has many positive health benefits. Vanity is healthy when used as a means to an end, given self-esteem is high. We should accept who we are and be happy with what life has blessed us. The rest is up to us. Vanity is not linked with exercise in my view, which is highly important, because fitness is linked with good health.

2.7.3.3.1 Public Environments

When I enter a social environment, I enter a charged-state where image stakes are on plank, which makes me say or do things that go against my nature. As if my instincts kick into play to make myself look the best I can in front of others… truth is, everyone is flawed. We become deathly afraid to share our inhibitions even though that is where our connections exist. That is, no one is perfect, and we can relate better if we realize everyone has some flaws. This cold eliminates self-esteem issues. Just chill, we're all 'bed-wetters', some later than others, it's how we learn and improve. Showing only the best version of ourselves to others is something that stems from the societal structures we are born in. For us to elevate this self-conscious state we need to realize we all have common ground.

Being aware of the humbling effect of death can influence how you reach your ideal self. When younger and sometimes even now I fight change and get upset when something doesn't go my way in group environments. I can build an attitude of negativity and sometimes act out in a way that is not productive or rightful. Often, it's only after the heat of the moment passes do I reflect on my actions that I wish things went differently. Apologizing is a crucial human skill that everyone needs to be genuinely aware of. An empty apology is bland and creates animosity. Societal structures were developed to give leaders an air of public superiority, which in general fosters animosity. Are we as a race being led by groups of individuals who have succumb to the pleasures of public status, and have lost sight of the true needs of a moral society?

2.7.3.3.2 Attraction

A power tool for many people. Studies have shown that people deemed attractive often have symmetrical facial features and are more likely advance through their careers. Physical attractiveness is a powerful tool and knowing how to apply vanity can have a large psychological influence in people around you. People who use this to manipulate others will often provide a sense that the person has a chance at a romantic future. Both men and women can use this charm to manipulate, and many are already aware of it. Yet, when caught in the moment rationale can escape us. Physical attraction is so powerful that empires have be destroyed and epics written over it.

2.7.3.3.3 Personality Imaging

A vast majority of people spend considerable time developing their public image. This can be observed in social interactions in high school. That was when I first took notice to the dramatic mental change of being at school and being at home, as everyone does at around that age. I started to care about how I looked and appeared to other people for the first time. Some are more comfortable than others in public settings, but it is not that everyone cannot become comfortable in public settings. Labels like extravert and introvert are psychological self-limiting boundaries that should not have been conceptualized. If we are to label ourselves it should be as in-progress, dynamic, and if anything, inexperienced, otherwise, labeling is a form of separation and self-limitation.

In public settings, all parties attempt to boost their appeal, while all are self-conscious of themselves. So how well do we know each other? Of course, this is easier said about two people who have equal levels of wealth and power status; which, normally accompany each other. When the level of wealth is different, there are more clear differences in who is the one trying to appear a certain way. We want to feel the equal to our friends. The differences in how much money people have dictate who they will hang out with and be friends with. Money has become many people's personalities. Many of us can easily be grouped together who make the same amounts of money. Especially, in their activities.

Why do we want people to perceive us a certain way? At a fundamental level, it appears to be recognition, but people treat others on bias views. For example, I hypothesize that if someone believes negative stories about another individual, they will be negatively bias against them in most cases regardless of whether it is justified and they discover it at later point or not. Knowing the un-justification does not completely rid the first negative bias. So, for best benefits to society we should never talk about people and situations when all parties are not present to defend themselves.

What I notice often of social interactions, are people boasting their materialistic accomplishments. All image building stuff. Yet, there exists great opportunity for self-growth if instead of talking about dated accomplishments or materialistic aspects of ourselves, we could reflect with each other our short-comings and downfalls, so everything is out in the open. However, it's the judgmental minds of people that scare us from sharing our thoughts. The truth is many people can immediately tell when someone is attempting to image boost themselves. When this happens, the image builder will likely suffer their image. Honesty, openness, and transparency are the best policies for self-improvement. I cannot emphasize enough how incredible the miracle of life is and that the mere fact of use standing here and breathing this air created by such a complex process that we need to prove nothing to anyone. We need only to accept and improve genuinely.

2.7.3.3.4 Pride

Many of us think of ourselves highly in our minds. We may also look down on others when, we think we are correct about an objective fact and they are not, but like in every sort of competitive environment, everyone starts a beginner. We should apply the same sort of competitive principle in this case that anyone would in any competitive scenario. Being competitive is beneficial to both parties; the losing side gets to improve by competing with someone more skilled, and the winner improves their game by giving away their tactics, eventually forcing their repertoire to grow.

A problem appears when we put people down based on subjective opinions on uncertain likelihoods. Even if we come out correct, we likely should maintain the same rational levelheadedness that likely got us to be correct in the first place. I've seen pride make men do crazy irrational things by blinding them from what is right in front of them. Sure-as-hell happened to me, when one particular woman attempted to take me for all I had. Often when we come up with a conclusion, it becomes personal and can be very difficult to pry away. We hate being wrong like I was about that woman. We hold on to losing stocks or failing businesses longer that we should, because by selling we admit we were wrong. Being wrong seems to be one of the most dreadful things we go through, which needs to change. Trial and error got us here in the first place. Many entrepreneurs learn early in life, that making mistakes and being wrong is part of life and should be embraced. Not only in the line of starting companies, but in every aspect of life, we need to stop being so worried and take those leaps. Outliers are a major component of innovation. Yet, societal structures suppress the creation of them through economic control of the money supply on top of over-regulation and bureaucracy.

At a very early age, education creates an authoritarian figure which was manifested from the pride of the original warrior kings of ancient times. We are conditioned to adhere to an authority and taught that a third party is always correct about things, when the reality is those adults doing the teaching are just as flawed as anyone else. They may be drinking too much at home due to their own problems or carry bias prejudice with an air of superiority over the pupil. All possibilities of which no one would generally be the wiser. This is anti-evolution, and after thousands of years has likely rooted deeply into our genetics. If this continues, it is likely that genuine leaders and critical thinkers will manifest less and less. Look at one of the most vital of thinkers, Isaac Newton. Not the type who took an authority's information. He instead took a leap and challenged himself to answer questions that changed the way our species understood the universe. Possibly being the person with the most influence over progress to date.

2.7.4   Self-Limitation

Self-limiting beliefs are a hindrance, which makes it crucial to teach our youths this concept early. We should believe we can access more than we allow ourselves. Societal structures have become societies collective self-limiting belief system that holds back our species from evolving to a point where we can expand beyond earth. My girlfriend always puts others needs above her own. That's why I love her so much. We had a conversation the other day about being taken advantage of at work. She was working at her job for two years, and they strung her along with the promise of a raise for five months and ended up giving her much less than she asked for. The time waiting for the raise made her content for getting anything at all and felt like a blatant manipulation of her emotions. Her self-limiting belief was placed in that she perceives bosses as authority figures and won't fight for her rights the way a union would. Rather, bosses at a place of employment should be teammates that work with someone rather than having employees feel like subordinates. Many fall into self-limitation because we are bred with an education system that is run and operated like a for-profit corporation, instead, of a needs-based non-corporate entity that can be created; given we use the needs-based monetary system I later outline in this book.

Our worst practice is self-limitation because any attainable goal is achievable. The combination of habit and subconscious self-limitation mechanisms lead us into rigid belief systems, which make it easy to fall into 'tunnel vision,' that limits creativity and the potential for innovation. In a person's personal life, these self-imitating believe systems will stop us from doing many things; especially, if they're challenging.

2.7.4.1 *Habits*

Many don't notice their habits, which can be compulsory. It seems logical that if one genuinely changes what they believe about habits, that belief would influence how they form habits. Understanding that habits are dynamic is a fundamental belief system required for the highest benefits to society. First, we should create firm belief systems, which should slowly remold how our brains work. If we reinforce the belief that habits are hard to break, our minds will form as such. How easy is it to remold belief systems? As a child, it is easy and malleable, and we should hold the same for adults if we want our brains to form this way. Because our habits and beliefs start forming when we are young, our childhood should be a disciplinary time of our lives of intense development of the mind and body if we want the best results from evolution. Instead, we have the opposite in place. Childhood is seen as a time of innocence and fantasy when our kids believe in fairy tales.

Belief itself is a form of habit. The more we reinforce our beliefs internally, the more it is likely to ring true. Once a habit is established or way of life determined, they become difficult to change, because we don't like admitting we're wrong. Concepts such as sayings like 'don't change what works," are critically weak, because if you have something better, why not? This saying, like many reduced sayings, do not work uniformly. However, they may apply in some cases. If there is anything to learn from history, it's that change is good and being wrong is a learning opportunity. Societal structures can be described as the moldings of societal habits. It creates good habits like that of reading and bad ones like that of keeping people down.

Our brains enjoy structure and end up fulfilling it through developing habits. If we are not careful which habits our minds attach themselves to, we may find ourselves down dark paths. Knowing what's going to happen provides security. Habits can form from uncertainty avoidance at one level, while at another they can develop from accomplishment, and they ingrain further every time the habits are re-performed. Understanding habits and how they form and affect our lives is something that children should be taught at a very young age. Especially habits regarding their health.

2.7.4.2 *Three-day Rule*

In my own life, I have set a three-day rule, that if I can do or not do something for three days in a row, my mind accepts it as a habit. A further note, from the belief system view, any limit of days could be set. Do our beliefs create fundamental connections that influence the way our brain forms habits? This could simply be the power of belief at work. I have at some point accepted three days to be true for me; therefore, it has been reinforced many years in my life. I experience the effect of the three days with my running exercises. If I can likely shoulder the energy to run for three days in a row, it will often set in motion a habit of running, and I have gone for over eight hundred days in a row off the first three days. I have realized since that taking days of rest, to me, applies to exercise only. Even then, a light exercise always does me well.

Teaching kids how to program these kinds of self-limits is crucial for their best development and our future advancements, because the responsibility will eventually be on them. Learning to program our subconscious belief systems and habits is like the foundation of a house, for the mind. By creating this early in our children's lives we greatly enhance their brain capacity for memory, fast learning, and critical thought. This will also greatly benefit evolution of the species brains. We are so obsessed with getting an AI or authority to do our thinking for us when we can naturally evolve ourselves into a super human race and it merely takes time and patience. Things modern brains are evolving to lack.

2.7.4.3 *Embarrassment*

The power of embarrassment is seen throughout the ages. From the times royals would force alleged criminals through the streets in mockery to today, when people are publicly humiliated by being branded criminals, and neglected by society. This type of punishment via embarrassment is no different than what we read about in historical classics like the Scarlet Letter. What is it that creates embarrassment? Being wrong? A callous can develop for that. It is the societal structure itself that creates embarrassment. In a pure society, no one would feel the need to be embarrassed. A concept would be eliminated from existence. Instead, embarrassment in society has been well established, even being used by religion in the form of sin.

Embarrassment is the central concept that formulates a pinnacle hierarchy. It relies on people feeling so embarrassed to the point which they bend to the rule of those above them, now considered those who have the most money. Embarrassment makes masses easy to control. The easiest form of ridicule to a person is to attack their financial status if lower than your own. What is this if not power over someone? This is an ingrained power point of control for those who are deemed old money. However, this is merely a perception and the public itself gives up power by allowing the fractional reserve system to exist. If we are too scared to be embarrassed of failing no one would every attempt anything, making it a self-limiting attribute. If we want to minimize self-limitation, we should minimize the role of embarrassment in our societal structures.

2.7.4.4 Compliance

Compliance to rules starts off when you are a kid and your mother told you not to touch the electrical socket. Of course, that kind of rule is established to benefit your well-being. What we have is a problem of compliance to authority in society. Is it a coincidence that religion also requires you to obey some sort of authority? What would a real free world look like? One that requires the bare minion compliance from people. Instead we need to open minds and encourage them to be creative. Compliance is one of the main things that limits us. How can we push limits if we are always compliant? If there were always compliance, we would never have developed anything. Compliance seems opposite of innovation.

2.7.5 Some Negative Behavioral Indicators – Results of Our Societal Structures

Today, societies structures carry several negative symptoms. A main issue being the failure to split needs-based goods and services from luxury-based goods and services. Today, we have a system that forces masses to sacrifice their dignities to survive, and people struggle. Free markets do not work as they would theoretically.

Human psychology and behavior is largely, if not fully, deterministic, and a major part of what determines our lives are societal structures. By looking at the negative aspects they produce, we see that there are still many negative outcomes. Yes, it has improved some standards of living through technology, but here I present a few social indicators of the much need adjustments to our societal structures.

2.7.5.1 *Fear*

Fear is dynamic and concentrates itself. We see how fear is used by politicians to influence elections in their favor. Terms like 'war-time presidents' are established. Fear is a tool for those who have power because it gives them absolute rule that is fueled by emotional fallacy. Whether it be war based or economic in nature there is always a garden variety of fear-based approaches a politician can take to influence voters in a debt-based fractional reserve run system. Why do we live in a world with societal structures that produce, suffering, war, and starvation? If you live in a first world country, well you might have to look a little harder to notice the worst of fears that exist around the world. You will not be preview to this. The reason first world countries are the way they are is because they have an economic hold on third world countries and global exchange rates.

We see how fear is used in the police force against the public itself. Countless police incidents in America where innocent people die and nothing happens to the officers. I'm not saying we don't need law enforcement, what I am saying is that we need to reconsider using fear tactics as a means of it. This is a topic that requires further analysis, but we see how the police force contributions to the idea of our society are fear-based. Follow our rules or suffer the consequences. When perceived from a dark moral perspective, fear is something you want to keep people in if they are your captives. You want them to be afraid to revolt and change the power structure. Fear is what child kidnappers do. Fear is a tactic you use if you yourself are fearful of up losing what you have.

A world in which fear is used to influence the masses is indictor of the conscious mentality of the people we have in power. Actions reveal the mentality of the actor. Today, we have groups of wealthy individuals who form conglomerates in the forms of clubs and societies in order to protect their positions. To people with such wealth, the world becomes a game of how to keep their wealth. That leads to populations being coerced into a perpetual mental state of fear to secure the power of a few.

2.7.5.2 *Depression*

Everyone is unique and the reasons for depression can vary vastly. Yet, the concept of depression itself is interesting as a belief system. If we did not have the word, we would simply describe it as sadness. As people who are miracles of survival, we can take our temporary time here for granted when we spend it in sad states. A BPR statistics report claims 74% of those who visited their doctors in the UK about depression were prescribed medication. I believe a leading cause of depression comes from the debt-based monetary supply systems that we have implemented.

2.7.5.3 *Addictions*

In today's world addictions run amuck, not only in an illegal market, but a legal one. People feel sad and take a happy pill. Again, these are symptoms of the lack of purpose the current societal structures place on humans. Addictions happen when people don't learn practical methods of developing habits and beliefs from an early age.

2.7.5.4 *Psychopaths*

I've heard claims that one in a hundred people are psychopaths. From what I understand, those psychopaths are deemed to be at the extreme of a spectrum that includes a variety of traits, and we all fall-in somewhere along that spectrum. We can tell that a lot of these traits are the same that are required for the government aspects of society. They are also largely the same as the ones needed for corporate success today.

2.7.5.5 *Mass Shootings*

Mass shootings are symptoms of bad competition and social status oppression. People want to feel superior, and likely for those people who commit these atrocities, it is their way to feel that superiority on people who they likely blame for some highly charged event in their lives which molded a negative belief in their minds that festered. More the reason to well teach our children from an early age about healthy competition principle. Being competitive is beneficial to both parties; the losing side gets to improve by competing with someone more skilled, and the winner improves their game by giving away their tactics, eventually forcing their repertoire to grow. The change and elimination of such symptoms may only come about after many generations of evolving in an appropriate manner. Of course, this is not to say that these are the only influences on mass shootings by the yare something that exist in our world today.

2.7.5.6 *War*

By far the worst symptom we see of the current societal structures is war within the species. Anti-productive killing of our own kind. Instead of waring we could be building and farming. This is the ultimate act of separation and divide. Yet, we do it in the name of profit. That thing called greed that grows from bad competition and the money's influence over psychology. This is a symptom deriving from government and religion that can be fixed with my needs-based monetary supply system and political model.

2.7.6 Recognition

Behind everything we do, we all want to be recognized. When we're children, we want to impress our parents because it feels good when people acknowledge us. I, like others, know the need to be acknowledged well. In a world where people all feel this way, we compete for this need. For the best of the species, it follows that we should recognize each other at the level of acknowledgement. Always say hi to the people that you walk past, seems so basic; yet, few do it especially in a metropolis. An example of how unrecognition is structurally implemented is through the pyramid scheme of the work force. Let's use a restaurant example, where the dishwasher is a vital role, but often earns the least. Or contractors for carpentry. A friend of mine's father gets paid 25 dollars on his work, who has been a carpenter for over 30 years, and the contractor charges out 70 dollars for his work but pays him 25. He does it in the form of subcontracting down so the contractor makes no contributions for the employee and ends taking 45 dollars from himself, almost double what the person doing the work gets. This is not recognizing our fellow humans. Never forget that it takes cooperation to build an efficient business or society. We need one another if we are to continue for the longest possible amount of time in this existence. Creating separation between ourselves is detrimental to our progress and we likely should start recognizing that we all had a hand in bringing society to be. Not merely people we remember throughout history, but every single one of each of our ancestors. We are the survivors; the fighters. The ones whose ancestors fought tooth and nail through ups and downs to get us here. We all had a part in it. Isn't it time for everyone to be recognized?

A desire for recognition gets conditioned into our minds when our naturally condescending parents treat us as naïve children. Our brains mold toward eventual need for recognition beyond a naïve person. Because we grow aware of their attitudes which can become permanent into our adulthoods, we sense when others look down on us. This inferior feeling is mentally suppressive and can be psychologically damaging. When you feel yourselves having your humility stray from your being, think about how everyone human comes from a long line of ancestors and is a multimillion year old organism that has refined over millions of years.

Regardless of what anyone says, we can rest assured that we are only alive because we are the newest version of our ever-evolving selves, and we have all given millions of years to our natural evolution. We are our ancestors, let's treat our children as we would our reincarnated selves and be lucky that we, as our children, have a blank slate to start fresh new memories. On the off chance that as children we do still hold past memories that we are not aware of later in life, it would be due to the communication difference of our minds during early development. Likely those memories would not only be distant like a dream, our means of communicating it would be impossible.

Recognition itself requires an authoritarian perspective of things, because the pupil is looking for recognition from the higher authority. This top down approach can always be considered to be an authoritarian view. This can trace back all the way to hunter gatherer civilizations. We at first looked at who was the strongest, some tribes looked at the wisest for guidance. Shamans and priesthood. The advent of money changed that. Now we look to who has the most money. Though we should start looking to the wisest and most logical. We have to start giving all those an equal opportunity to speak and have their word no matter the age or credential because the subconscious mind is a powerful thing, we all have deep roots.

As hunter gatherers recognition was given to those who could provide for the tribe. Recognition likely should have has evolved since the very beginning and therefore is one of the most deeply impeded needs a human has within their genetic makeup. Great minds define their lives for the desire to achieve fame and make a mark in history. It drives people and their behaviors to pursue everything. It drives human behavior at the most fundamental level. No matter what we do, it is somehow linked to achieving recognition.

The human need for recognition is what drives innovation. Newton created calculus over trying to prove his intelligence in order to achieve intellectual recognition. Everything with moderation. Recognition can be something that is given to a Nobel prize winner who managed to improve human life and bring some kind of significant advancement. It can also come in form of wealthy children who simply want to feel better about themselves and can only do so in the spot light. They are very different kinds of recognition will have carry greatly in how they survive the test of time. We should recognize more people around us. We are all miracles in it of ourselves. You are a living miracle. We are surviving organisms that have been through plagues, wars, starvation, and famine to somehow survive countless tests of nature. Humanity still stands. Life is a gift, and we likely should cherish it in every single individual, because we all carry so much genetic history within us.

Today our societal structures take advantage of this need in humanity to place people at the top of an authoritarian power structure in charge of recognition. We hold recognition back from each other in our personal lives and work lives. Current societal structures fail to recognize people as part of the same species by creating divide between us. The economic system gives all the monetary supply power to a few people and sets it up in a fashion that does not serve the species but rather small groups of people. We have confined ourselves to strict societal structures that put a separation hindrance on our treatment of each other. No fault exists; rather only recognition of this issue is required to fix things. Instead, of anger toward it, we likely should recognize that it did work to get us here in the first place, but the time for improvement is now becoming long over do. Enough consequential indicators of our actions exist for us to recognize that we should be more proactive in securing our future existence. Need I recount historical morality and war?

Modern politics is the biggest form of false recognition we have to date. One becomes president with the help of many and takes credit for running a country. It is a popularity contest for the rich that relies on the influence money now has over minds. They run campaigns completely from a self-serving point of view. They care only for the image that appeals to the mass mentality of people. Whatever fits their objective is what they do. Most politicians want personal recognition, but that's it. Very few ever truly desire to improve nations. Most of the time they are rich kids with no perspective on the general populace.

In fact, normally they are likely to look on the general public in a negative fashion. However, they will never reveal that in public. The problem is that these rich kids have, from an early age, been exposed to a life were everyone gives them a sense of unjustified recognition. They get to experience this from mostly anyone that is of a deemed 'lower wealth class' or social class then they are. Depending on their parents, they may or may not get recognition from them, so they will seek to maximize their parent's full recognition. They will chase this throughout life. What some don't understand is that the genuine recognition they desire will likely never be achievable, because people who never know what it is to truly struggle for survival will never get recognition from those who struggle for survival. This is at the basic fundamental nature of humanity; to survive. If we cannot experience the struggle for survival, we, by most human definitions, are an underdeveloped person still feeling the protection of 'security'. Struggle for survival build and reveals true character. Like what you would do in a dire circumstance… many of us never get the privilege of this discovery and may behave as children do in a chocolate factory.

3 RELIGION

"Assuming you know an uncertainty may be pleasant but accepting that you don't know is realistic."

3.1 FAITH

If faith convinces a person to suicide bomb themselves, killing innocent people, what is more powerful than faith? Getting someone to believe in something without any evidence is absolute power over their mind. Charlatan preachers publicly trick audiences on TV and pretend to cure them with miracles. Who knows... maybe there's a placebo effect... however, I believe faith is fundamentally misunderstood as a concept. Assuming that something is fact without evidence is a recipe for ignorance. The only good use of faith comes when accomplishing goals that are plausible. Like having faith that you will reach the end of your Ph.D.

Never taking faith on unproven ideas, such as the afterlife or whether there is a creator, is rational. Adding a consequence to the rejection of such a belief is coercive power... and basically, extortion. Religious faith in some minds boils down to an invented super being holding a gun to our heads telling us how to behave, or we will be severely punished for eternity. Funny how religion is an authoritarian belief system, and so are the political and monarchical systems throughout history. This is no coincidence at all. Belief systems are incredibly amazing in controlling mass mentality, but who are they mostly benefiting? When you take something universal that everyone fears like death and provide an answer, people confide in you. Someone likely should have caught on to this power early in oral tradition and used it to their benefit, and today many still fall for the same old tricks. Just a reminder, faith in the ideas of others over the uncertainty of death is not a rational concept.

Faith, when misused is counterproductive, as in, if you accept things in faith, you risk to not look for plausible solutions to uncertainty. Are we as a race going to have faith that a super being will prevent the world from being destroyed by volcanoes or a massive asteroid? I hope not, because we are highly likely the only creatures around who can understand science and natural reality enough to make a difference when the time comes. Had we not grown up with the concept of faith misconstrued in our collective subconscious, we may not so quickly fall for the trickery used by politics in producing votes for themselves, Nigerian scams, or fortune-telling today. I find it highly likely it is the misuse of faith that has allowed for a naïve population to evolve or at least a good portion of them.

3.2 THEOLOGY

3.2.1　Divinity

God is defined in monotheistic religions as a creator and ruler of the universe and source of all moral authority, the supreme being. A divine being in itself is mythological in nature, and we see human image portrayed in the monotheistic depiction of God. They say God made people in his image, but God itself is a concept created by the human mind while trying to answer questions about natural disasters and philosophical issues.

Because we mold physical material, we assume it likely should be a quality of God or that a being with this quality is responsible for our creation. Our collective conscious desires a creator for the universe because it gives us an answer while the phenomenon of the universe may or may not require a creator at all. We are a product of the natural environment without question, not the creation of a being in a direct sense because our parents created us. It is in our heads that the universe needs a creator or ruler, this is not something that is naturally required. It is us who needs that to be true, not the universe. Like God, divinity is a human created concept, something placed upon the world without any evidence that it exists. Instead what ancient texts like the Vedas or the Torah attempted to teach us was the civil order that would best lead to our ultimate survival. They are meant as practical texts.

What the monotheistic god is, is morality itself. This is what was right about theology. It allowed for us to slowly develop morality; as famously quoted in Luke 6:31, 'do to others as you would have them do to you.' However, the authoritarian concept of a supreme God is the double edge of the sword, because it is contradictory to the golden rule, and it enables immoral societal structures. It allows for leaders who realize the power and use of these structures to maintain control via the monetary system. This authoritarian belief system creates people who live in supreme power and turn their heads in the face of poverty without true efforts at a solution, which allows our leaders to not do on to others as they would have done to them unless they wouldn't mind their own actions against them had they been born into poverty.

The study of creation is different than the study of the afterlife. A creator or ruler would really only be required by the universe at one time. That is, when the universe is created. What would be the need for the creator post creation, as we have seen nature to be autonomous but also unjust and a-moral to our standards. If a creator is watching, that creator has no sympathy for living beings. The study of morality and the possibility of spirit is vastly more intriguing.

3.3 WHEN WE DIE, THE WORLD CONTINUES.

3.3.1 What end?

There is peace in accepting uncertainty. It relaxes the brain to focus on living life. That does not mean I believe that nothing will exist when we die or that there is no creator for certain. First of all, what is nothing? Can there be more than one concept of nothing? Could there be more to this journey than this earthly physical plane of experience? I imagine there is, but who knows… ☺

First of all, the belief that there is nothing can be easily proven wrong in a sense, since we know that when we die the world continues. Therefore, when we die, there is still something, it is merely the end of our individuality. What we wonder, is what happens to our relative conscious. Well, if we have children, we literally pass physical cells onto that child and with that create a new conscious. We all think of reincarnation as a hypothetical concept, but, because we see it so often, we have grown accustomed to what it is. Every day, when someone is born, that is us reincarnating in quite a physical sense. Yet, we all create an idea of what it should be, when it sits right before our eyes. The proof is in the pudding. Well, the proof that we continue is in our offspring's DNA. Quite literally.

When we die, our children represent a new conscious continuation and is still present in the world. Because we live concurrently with our offspring, we cannot feel their conscious due to separate bodies, but it is possible that you reawaken in your children's body without a direct awareness of it, like how dreams aren't remembered. This is a simple argument to make for practical reasons.

When passing our DNA to our children, we have a connection that continues with them as we did with our ancestry. We are one organism. There is no death without the death of the species. On another note, we could simply be derivatives from the earth itself. If the earth is conscious then we are merely byproducts and indeed possibly tiny extensions from its conscious state. I do not claim to know what happens after death, for I alone, can come up with endless alternate hypothesis'.

When a person claims to accurately guess what afterlife is or if there is a creator, it is complete hubris simply because of the infinite amount of possibilities. Taking into account the computation of possibilities that exist for the afterlife, we likely should accept the probability of any one person guessing or any single possibility being correct, to be infinitely against us. Since the concept of 'nothing' is only one possibility in an infinite sequence of them, the chances of them being correct are the same as any other. That being one divided by the number of possibilities, which I'm sure you can imagine is an infinitely small number. To me faith in any one of those singular possibilities is like a person placing a dollar on a roulette table with infinite numbers and claiming that it will land, so basically complete nonsense.

3.4 PERSPECTIVE BEFORE COMMON ERA

3.4.1 Viewing Lenses

A strange phenomenon occurs when a person knows something and they expect the other person to also know what they know. They automatically assume others understand it the way they do. This phenomenon shows itself in a different way when we look back in time. It can be tough for us to place ourselves in the perspective of the people of the era. We expect them to have our understandings. That's why people will read about Robinson Crusoe or the witch trials in disgust, but back in the time, it would be controversial to say such things nor did those ancestors feel that way. Makes it more difficult for us to put ourselves in the moral perspective of someone living in those times, and for us to think back on the people of the distant past, we likely should attempt to observe the evidence through their eyes.

3.4.1.1 Ancient Collective Memory

Without historical recordings, our ancestors had nothing to go on but what the oldest person could recount. So, we had dedicated classes that would recite these stories. If you lived with a small hunting band, you might have known nothing but the road behind the game you were tracking. There were collective memories but not many, mainly practical trade knowledge of hunting and gathering.

3.4.1.2 Morality

In the common era, our ancestors were developing the best form of morality to suit survival. We were a-moral at best. Killing for anyone alive during this period was second nature and likely a practiced skill. Cooperation started morality… realizing we are stronger united. The bible depicts how life was seen at the time of its authors, and we have early accounts such as Abel and Cain. These were the early thoughts of morality. It could also be seen as the first thoughts of rationality or utilitarianism. The first realizations of 'the betterment of unity.' We were still figuring out that we should not kill each other. Something nations still struggle with around the world today.

3.4.1.3 *Time*

The concept of measuring time was only just beginning and not many people understood it. It was an unrecorded era. People lived day by day without the concept of years or weeks. They merely lived out each cycle of the sunlight and the seasons. History was not known and there was no concept of how old the world was.

3.4.1.4 *Geography*

Maps had not been developed, so no understanding of continents or placement was conceptualized. Some knew how to navigate using the stars but often it was likely known to few and mainly used to track food. People knew paths and large points of reference to get around as they migrated so they had some sense of direction.

3.4.1.5 *Communication*

Written letters did not exist. It was basically what you could get across when you saw the person or messengers. Family ties and unions were likely at its infancy. Imagine running an empire this way? Not going to be easy.

3.5 STORY 10,500-6,500 BCE

3.5.1 Oral Tradition

Before writing, we were storytellers, passing knowledge and wisdom down through enchanting mythological creations. During this period, we were influenced by encounters with wild beasts and natural disasters. Dedicated elders recalled stories of the past, which likely explained natural disasters as acts of supreme entities rather than natural events. Long-term systems and structures could not be created because we had the collective memory of single individuals, which led to bias ideologies and stories being told of creation and the nature of things. We quickly distorted our history as generations died and stories of past were exaggerated. We all know the telephone game where we pass a message to the next person and by the end of it, the message has been distorted beyond recognition. Our ancestors only kept what was practical and relevant to survival in their environment.

In ancient times, our most common encounters were with wild beasts, and we all know the fisherman's story of the ever increasingly large fish. Well, I don't doubt the same thing happened back then; people told their stories and, as time passed, these stories of natural beasts and humans became miss construed by bards of the time… even the outcomes themselves. These stories led to the creation of myths and wild superstitions, most of which can be explained by science today had we been witness to the events.

As people died, older stories were told by elders with secondhand accounts. They likely modified the story for maximum effect and so accuracy was saturated. But new listeners who learn the stories from third, fourth, and further accounts of the ones who experienced it, likely developed wild comprehensions that stretched far from the truth.

3.5.2   Doggerland and Storegga Slide 6225-6170 BCE

Doggerland was an area now beneath the southern North Sea that connected Britain to Europe. Flooding occurred during a 300-year period and ended with the Storegga landslide, which submerged settlements equivalent to the size of Iceland under 34 M of water. (Coles, n.d.) In its final stages, the Storegga slides created a final tsunami in the North Atlantic Ocean.

Doggerland's destruction likely should have created ballads that would have traveled back to Mesopotamia, the center of commerce around the time, having been situated at the crossroads of Africa, Europe, and Asia. This is most likely the origin of all flood myths. Anyone living in Doggerland at the time, with their perspectives, witnessed their lands disappear over a handful generations. The last ones living there would slowly have grown accustomed to the fact that they happened, likely building boats during times leading up to flooding. As far as their eye could see the world was covered in water and likely many got out in fishing boats and went on to tell heroic stories escaping the grasp of the gods. Rulers at the time of Storegga who were not affected by the landslides would likely have heard and possibly met with survivors, for whom they would have created ballads.

These stories would have over 2000 years of distortion by oral tradition. Enough time for people of that era to lose track of accuracy and details. When script first came about, these stories were still being told, though likely manipulated by the first priest-kings. The perspective of time is crucial in this analysis, because then, people had no notion of how old the world was. After a few generations those who knew the floods happened during their lifetime died, and there was nothing to prove to following generations that those accounts did not in fact occur across the entire world. Today we can easily look back and prove that in fact it was a centralized event, but back then it could have easily been misconstrued through time without scripture.

3.5.3 Importance of Natural Disasters

Forces exist that threaten all of us. Earthquakes, volcanoes, asteroids, and tsunamis have played a role in the humanities unity. Natural disasters likely should have impacted people so greatly that it was embedded into oral tradition. The immense power of natural disasters brought people together and sent them in search of explanations. These large events likely should have scared the tribes into working closer together and uniting themselves in fear of these events they blamed on the supernatural. Disasters are what led to the cooperation of humanity. They taught us the world can end. These events of doom brought us together and likely is responsible for the first concepts of religion, which was the beginning of societal structures. Religion in its advent was the first form of science being that it tried to explain natural events.

3.5.4 Polytheism

Polytheism, or paganism, as referred to Yehezkel Kaufmann, was the a-moral view of the world that developed during the oral tradition period. Polytheism claims a meta divine realm which can be influenced with magic rituals. Everything is explained through these forces of nature, which are in their view gods. They believe that humans could influence the gods and that gods themselves are not alive forever, but instead, they live long lives compared to humans and are born like humans from sexual intercourse. Gods have a very human image in polytheism; though, are mythological in nature and may have alternate forms like the gods of Hinduism.

To me it was likely that ancient priests pretended to be divine and as time passed, others believed them. Imagine early on what someone could do if they were a natural illusionist or got lucky enough to time a magic ritual with the weather in front of others? I believe certain humans conned others to believe that they were gods, which mixed into oral tradition giving the Polytheistic view of gods a human quality. Such an elder wise-person would predict the weather and season accurately for the group, while the rest of the group may not know how they did it because likely it was from age and experience. This is where I believe humanization of the Polytheistic god comes from. With the nature of collective memory, we had none still so group and community dynamics likely should have dramatically changed as generations changed. With Polytheism we are left the mental artifacts of our past oral traditions.

3.5.4.1   Comparison to Monotheism

The similarities are numerous when comparing the two religions, where both contain ritual practice, and also share a lot of the same stories and myths. The truth is that our current religions hardly differ from the old religious views of ancient oral tradition. Kaufmann mainly points out the major differences as summarized below.

3.5.4.1.1 Limitations of the Gods

Gods in polytheism were limited in their power. They were constrained to their specific duties in nature. This was almost a scientific view of things, but rather than seeing these as autonomous forces without a conscious, we had the need of giving them a conscious to make them more like ourselves.

3.5.4.1.2 Mythology

Mythology is the pagan scientific reason whether correct or not. The use of story to explain natural disasters.

3.5.4.1.3 Evil

According to Kaufmann Evil in Polytheism is built into the structure of the universe. This idea leads to people believing that they are not accountable for their actions, but instead, that evil forces drive humans to do evil deeds. Sounds a little like determinism to a certain degree.

3.5.4.1.4 Meta divine Realm

The belief that there is a meta divine realm exists and connects the human world with that of the gods. There is a fluid boundary between all realms. the gods are bound to this meta divine realm, and we humans have influence over it through ritual use.

3.6 SUMER AND MESOPOTAMIA 5100-500 BCE

3.6.1 Unity is the best form of Survival

The first groups of people likely formed after accumulating stories of world-ending natural disasters inspired the creation of powerful myths that enabled a priest-class to rule large groups of believers in their word. Being few, that were in charge of keeping the collective memory, it was easy for them to manipulate others to their whims. From the advent of civilization, the masses have been conditioned for authoritarian structures. Individuals have always shaped the species beliefs into societal structures that mostly benefit a handful at the top.

This was a unique era of our history as it was the first time everyone was afraid of the same natural powers. The concept that something we did not understand was out there and could wipe us out brought humanity together and allowed commerce to exist. Being an area with a high activity of trade and fertile farmlands, Sumer and Mesopotamia, now in modern-day Iraq, prospered. Populations grew to unprecedented levels and the need to track trade led to writing. This unity allowed for society to flourish and by that time, stories of Storegga would have been distorted into some sort of creation myth along the lines of the Epic of Gilgamesh.

3.6.2 Babylon 2300-500 BCE

In Babylon, religious structure corresponded precisely with the social structures of Mesopotamian society. They had a pyramid structure like the ones we still use today. Why? Because it followed from the old classes of the priest-kings who had established a set of beliefs. The fear of death allowed for the priest class to control the minds of others. Slowly, over new generations, practical military minds took over these priest-kings. They likely should have realized the use of keeping the masses brainwashed under a belief system structured to benefit the ruling class. Let's not forget this was a time when murder and slavery was common. More evidence we need to re-consider the Pyramid structure of things.

It was in Babylon that originated the creation Epic of Enûma Eliš and the Epic of Gilgamesh. These were the first stories to be written into clay tablets that had survived the bumpy ride of oral tradition. Here we have the first encounters with the Garden of Eden, the advice from Ecclesiastes, and the Genesis flood narrative. These epics were compilations of countless stories that survived oral tradition. That is simply it. Not the word of a divine being, but the word of exaggerated practical experience.

The ancient near east mentality was that of barbaric savages who cared little for the concept of utilitarianism. Instead, rulers served themselves by pure manipulation of the mind of others with religious teachings. I say teachings because it is difficult to know for sure whether the rulers were true believers of morality or whether they simply used it for the practical reasons of self-gain. It is no mystery that manipulation and secrecy have played a factor in human history.

Within their depiction of reality, humans are slaves to gods, likely a belief that derived from the occurrence followed by the depiction of catastrophic natural events as punishments of humanity. But, they also believe that certain humans have a connection to these gods so basically making lower classes also servants to these special humans at the top. How self-serving is that? This likely happened because such cataclysmic events happen rarely and after a few generations from the original, new generations of priest may not have considered them real events anymore. They begin to doubt the reality of God. Things like this until at the next big disaster occurs striking belief back into the clergy.

The problem was that people were led to believe that they could influence the gods in Polytheism. This sort of structure allowed for uprising and civil unrest over natural events. It was not stable enough of a belief system for large populations to be ruled by few rulers. However, it could also have been that the ruling classes were non-believers. A question I would surely like the answer to. Likely they believed the stories themselves, which made them that much more convincing.

3.7 EGYPT 3500-50 BCE

3.7.1   Pyramid Texts 2400-2300 BCE

These are the oldest religious texts known to man and date back to 2400-2300 BCE. Writing had finally allowed for the standardization and a consistency to religious belief. Those belief developers were the tail end of oral tradition in their region. So, here we have an early concept of the afterlife that is dramatically different than the ones today. Again, like Babylon we see a highly authoritarian priest-king pyramid structure of classes. A hierarchy which likely caught on and stuck because of its use in controlling large groups of people.

With Egyptian culture, we see how they incorporated religious belief into their social order. Egyptian kings of this time had up to three titles, the Horus, The Nesu Bety, and Nebty; official intermediaries between the people and the gods. The first use of standardized religion was to enslave countless people and set them to work on the Pyramids. Religion was more a social structure that served an authoritarian purpose than truth-seeking thought at this point with the Horus playing the roulette game of the afterlife with odds infinitely against him. After such an idea has been placed, new generations born into their existence have no reason to doubt what they are conditioned to. The beginning of population control.

This was an afterlife-based theology. We see here the first use of religion to be to serve the authority of the time solely through fear of the afterlife. These were modern times of tyranny, and likely had a lot of civil disturbances. This use of religion counters the golden rule and treats humanity as not inherently equal of rights.

3.7.2   Book of The Dead 1550 BCE – 50 BCE

Funny thing about the coffin texts is that it came about because of the demand from the noble classes for afterlife creation. The trend caught on... this spoke of a 'Duat' or underworld where it was meant to be the realm of the dead. Osiris being the ruler or deity of this realm. Here we have the first concept of the modern-day hell and the introduction of ruling by fear.

3.8 PROGRESSION OF WRITING 1ST MILLENNIUM BCE

3.8.1   A New Collective Memory

Writing itself was seen as digressive for the mind in its beginning and likely was correct as we notice brain sizes shrinking in the last ten thousand years. Socrates, was worried about the development of human memory capacity, suggesting an early basic understanding of evolution of the mind. Indeed, visualization and memory technique in the masses has greatly decreased. It was the first time that generations had real access to past knowledge without the telephone game effect of distortion. They could finally pass down information and build on it through experimentation. This was technically the first true tool of the scientific method for our race. Being able to keep track of information beyond our physical memories, and without distortion bias. The script was finally stable but only by the last authors who had written them.

Writing was the major advent, it gave us a collective memory at the cost of our individual memories if we neglect them. A databank of information. A way to keep ideas and concepts going with accurate detail. This would have likely derived from the need of traders trading goods back and forth in a city like Babylon where trade was huge. Together with currency. As writing become more widespread, teachings were being compiled into collections from people of varying fields from morality, to politics, and ethics.

3.9 JUDAISM 9TH CENTURY BCE

3.9.1   24 Books of the Tanakh 4th century BCE

Judaism finds its roots in the Bronze age and derives from the polytheistic religion of the Canaanites which originated from Babylon. Through history, there were no original copies of the work dating back before the common era. Not until the middle of the twentieth century did we discover the dead sea scrolls. This evidence proved this scripture in fact did originate in the 3rd and 4th century BCE. Some differences were apparent but enough correlations were made to accept them as the origin. Here we see evidence that these writings are not of a divine nature.

The group of Israelites who formed the Torah in the 3rd and 4th century BCE imposed their worldview on the on-going belief systems of the time to form monotheism. Some scholars believe the books were a product from the Babylonian captivity of the Kingdom of Judah, which makes a whole lot of sense. It seems likely from a psychological perspective, that a captive person will be open to see the pure good in things and bound themselves to morality because they are the victims of tyranny and pure narcissistic hate of the old religions which were established by priest-kings to benefit the upper classes. It would be difficult for someone of that kind of ruling class to intuitively understand the concept of morality as they are born into a world where they see themselves as better and not equal to others by divine right. Especially, when rulers were born into complete power and domination over others through false belief systems.

These men who wrote the initial scripture likely should have gone through misery and seen their people suffer and the injustice that comes with the greed of mankind. I don't know about you, but I can see how a person going through that sort of struggle would develop such ideas of morality and the golden rule. Yet, we still see the authoritarian structure of a greater being that encompasses all. A belief system that molds its believers to look up to a single entity seems authoritarian in nature still. This leads me to believe that people who are born into wealth have a lessened capacity for morality and instead, have to work harder for it not to be merely a desire for the image of morality. For a person to truly be a moral one, they likely should have experienced the suffering side of survival before they can really say they understand what sufferers go through. So, when choosing leaders, do not pick them over their wealth, pick the person who can relate to the people they are meant to represent. However, the societal structures likely should consider adjustments to the government aspects of how representation works in the twenty first century.

3.9.2 Yehezkel Kaufmann 1889 – 1963 CE

Monotheism has many similarities and ties to ancient

polytheism; therefore, evolved from polytheism. Instead of reflecting a ruling class's ideals it reflects the bottom classes ideals in its initiation. Biblical ties to the ancient eastern world are quite numerous. Scholars often point to these themes and plot similarities. On the other hand, scholars like Yehezkel Kaufmann argued that monotheism cannot evolve from polytheism. I cannot see this being true as the developers of monotheism would have been exposed and influenced by polytheism. Clearly using the ancient tales of oral tradition as source material for their ideas of creation.

Kaufmann's attempt at discrediting monotheism as evolving from polytheism does not follow as they both share the concept of creation. For monotheism to have been original, it would have had to precede the concept of polytheism altogether for which it does not. Polytheism likely came from the best attempts at rational explanations of natural disasters; thus, displays the characteristics of such. Monotheism originates not from the need to explain natural disasters, but the human struggle of mass slavery, and thus displays the characteristics of such. Both are two sides of the same concept and therefore one could not have come about without the other. Without the fundamental structure that polytheism created, monotheism would not have developed. Polytheism brought people together and allowed for societal structures to grow to the point of commerce and created slavery. Slavery in turn lead to the development of moral theology; therefore, does in fact derive from Polytheism.

People don't want their ideas to be the same as others and monotheism is different than Polytheism; though, it derives from it. These are two different matters. Kaufman claimed that they shared only with symbols and story but not function. Yehezkel Kaufman is simply trying to achieve a feeling of superiority over Polytheism, because it feels bad to be the second to something; especially, when the newer version is more morally just.

3.9.3   Monotheism vs Polytheism

The difference is that god in Monotheism is absolute and moral while Polytheism views gods as mortal and morality as ingrained into the fabric of the universe. The gods were natural forces that surround us. God is beyond nature in the Israelite view of things. God has no relationship to humans in the bible. Afterlife is more of a Polytheistic view of the world, which was re-incorporated later in time. The Hebrew Bible did not speak of an afterlife in its introduction. There is no meta divine realm in the bible. These differences display the nuisance's that a low social class would likely have come up with for freedom. Monotheism takes God's will as absolute. In the biblical view there are no evil beings and there is no realm of supernatural beings to fight God. Sin and evil are demythologized in their worldview. They do not believe there is an evil power that exists but it is the human nature and free will to act on it. A moral reality. Every human has the sole responsibility for their sins. However, as I have contemplated, free will may not be free at all.

3.9.4   Good, Bad, and Preservation

This takes the idea of leading by example into practice but we likely should understand that the concept of what is good is merely that, a concept. Humanity has a need to believe that the term 'good' and 'bad' have inherent natural means and significances in existence. These words are simply creations of the human mind to classify certain behaviors we generally agree or disagree with. Believing God is good by nature assumes that the concept of good and evil existed in the natural world before we evolved into modern humans. When it comes down to it, religion was all about self-preservation, because we understood at the fundamental level of survival as a race, we need to be 'good' to each other or else undesirable outcomes tend to occur. Good and bad are human creations and not relevant to any sort of energy source that may have created us. This notion of good derives from the survival benefits of cooperation. Cooperation has indeed led to the best results of our survival.

3.9.5   Provability

The one problem with Polytheism was that it was easily disproven in practical life. Objective and rational people of the time would have easily seen for themselves through practice that these beliefs were not reality. Monotheism attempts to make disproving it with critical thought more difficult. With the 24 books of Tanakh, that is what you get. An idea that is very difficult to prove right or wrong because of the removal of all things that would lead to us connecting with this supernatural belief.

3.9.6   Shifting power influencers

Along with this new school of thought came coinage. It was a major turning point in human history when political power and influence shifted from those with divine knowledge types to Imperial Powers who controlled material possessions. It set forth an economic system to coincide with religious belief systems.

3.10 EARLY CHRISTIANITY PRE-325 CE

3.10.1 Septuagint

One of the first translations of the Old Testament was into Greek and called the Septuagint for Jews in Alexandria, and Egypt during the 3rd century BCE. Some things were different in the translations including the order of the book, which splits its teachings into, past, present, and future, where Genesis through Esther tell of things past, Job through the Song of Solomon contains wisdom that applies to the present, and the rest tell of things future. Some copies contain additional books. This Septuagint later became the framework for the modern bibles of Christianity.

Christianity like Judaism hates the Pagan gods and denied all other gods other than their own. This was new because Polytheism accepts worship of different gods. It is the captive mentality that will build hate for all those of the belief that enslaved them.

3.10.2 Apostolic Age Approx. 33 CE – 100 CE

This was the age of the Apostles and the Christians began to follow Jesus Christ. The apparent rise of Jesus is supposedly around 33 CE. Christians of the time were mainly Jews. This was the period where Empires were first growing beyond the social structure limited by society without coinage. Coinage coinciding with Monotheistic Abrahamic religions clashed the power of belief and the power of economy with Rome and Judaism. In the past people knew that belief was the way to start a society. This was the first time in history that the old ways of setting up a society didn't work. At this point it was coinage which allowed for the rapid expansion of armies.

3.10.3 Origins of Modern Christianity in Rome 27 BCE – 395 CE

With Rome rapidly rising into the world's largest city, Judaism found its way into its culture. Through this era, it grew to the point in which it became a problem for the Roman Empire. By 324 CE, Constantine the Great, had achieved authority over the eastern and western kingdoms of the Roman empire. Constantine was the first to recognize the potential unification aspects of Christianity and decided to modify it to benefit his empire and went on to restructure the government and economy of Rome. He was the one to establish a Gold based coin.

Through Eusebius of Caesarea between the time periods of 311 – 314 CE, Constantine began tolerance for Christianity, likely over the social benefits of controlling growing populations. Though, as has been famously quoted, 'history is written by its successors.' I reckon that history has likely been rewritten at such stages, making it difficult to get a perfectly accurate account of what happened. I assume Constantine gathered his best philosophers and reformed the older teachings into a unified religion fit for their purpose, making Christianity a Roman adaptation of Judaism. Constantine was a person who desired stability for the Empire and used Christianity for political benefit of unifying the beliefs of mass populations. On his deathbed, it is claimed that he finally converted; likely, the fear of death got to him. I find it likely that true accounts of historical events were largely re-written during this period, as it was the first time power over such masses had become that centralized. Constantine studied and understood Christianity from a practical perspective without regard to the philosophical and moral views of it and likely saw it as a tool for control over his empire.

3.10.4 Bible

The bible was an anthology. It is a collective library of stories written by various authors throughout time. Many believe the bible is the word of God, but in the beginning, they were the passing down of ancient oral traditions. We have analyzed exactly where the bible came from, why it originated, the way it did, and in no way is it the word of something other than ancient experienced humans. It was until later that the idea that the bible is the word of god. At first it was developed orally and the story passed down and developed among the Israelites. Religion has foregone many changes and reformulations to better serve the survival of societies. This was in a way the first version of our historical documentation. People have turned religion into a self-serving institution.

3.11 ISLAM 570 CE – 632 CE

3.11.1 Origins

Islam is the most recent religion of the major Abrahamic monotheistic religions. Shares the same aspects of Christianity and Judaism, that they all have the same origins of ancient near east folklore. That is what it is, folklore. Old stories which likely hold mere fractions of truth to them. Islam also decided to modify their version of Judaism as the final word of God. A little nuisance or trick to try and play into the conversion of people. Islam takes the ideas of Judaism and modifies them so suit their culture in Mecca.

3.11.2 Qur'an

The Islamic Bible is seen as the word of God. All Abrahamic religions see their own views as the word of God. Solid evidence that none are likely to be correct as probability is infinitely against them. The Quran uses a lot of the same major narratives as the Bible, sometimes changing in some cases the accounts given. The Quran establishes firmly as a book of guidance for mankind. There are many indicators that this is an extension of the 24 books of Tanakh which had origins in Babylonian Polytheism, which can be found online.

3.12 FINAL WORDS ON RELIGION

3.12.1 Road Map

This chapter was meant as a very brief road map of how religion developed through the use of writing. I am by no means an expert in Theology. There are many details I have left out. For a more in-depth look at religious history I suggest doing further self-study. For the purposes of this book, this is enough to demonstrate the importance of religion in human progress and it's influences; being that religion is a societal structure. Don't hate me, but for religion, I acquired much of my information from Yale Online lectures off YouTube.

3.12.2 Separation of Morality and Theology

Surely almost everyone can agree on most moral aspects of many religions universally. Especially, at a fundamental level. What we likely should do is separate the idea that morality and theology are paired. These are two different things. By combining them, we allow for the corrupt use of religion to control masses by a few people. We can be moral beings without having to subscribe to infinitely improbable ideas of uncertainties regarding death and god.

3.12.3 Original Use

In the beginning religion was used to serve the controllers of it forming the Priest-Kings and has continued to serve rulers through the ages by establishing an authoritarian belief system in which the mass population would easily succumb to authority. Religion has been manipulated and rewritten to suit the most recent controllers of it. At first it was Polytheism inspired by natural events, then Babylonian captives took their form of Polytheism and changed its underlying concept of God in order to mock their captor's belief systems. It is no surprise that their belief system would completely deny their former systems in manner where slavery would be abolished by moral belief. These people wanted to free themselves. Though, we likely should praise that it allowed for the structuring of the first large cities of humans, we likely should re-consider its use in the twenty first century.

3.12.4 Iconic Aura

Rulers of ancient times likely realized that once the masses see you as an icon they act very differently to you. This now happens with money. The more money you have, people look at you as if you are divine because you have purchasing power of luxuries and needs. We see this aura take affect all the time with celebrities being harassed by fans everywhere they go. This is the iconic aura which early rulers established with use of myth and religion. This aura allowed for the early priest-kings to live and rule their groups without effort. We see a framework for the control of populations, but it is morality that unifies us, because it gives us common ground, which was crucial for pact survival.

3.12.5 Practical Use of Religion

The old Polytheist structures allowed for too many civil problems, because people believed they had influence in the order of existence. Not necessarily a bad belief. Monotheism destroyed this self-empowering belief system and implemented a fear-based afterlife one that would break down factions and unite belief.

3.12.6 Christmas Fact

In ancient times, Christmas was chosen on that day to ease the conversion of pagans to Christianity.

3.12.7 Past Intentions

The rules of the past had one thing in mind; to maintain their seed in power and wealth. Above that, they cared about leaving stories that would record them in history. To them it was the closest thing to immortality.

3.12.8 Separation of Morality and Religion.

With morality separate from religion, we are free to belief whatever ideas about afterlife and god while living in a moral world regardless of how improbable they are. I want to remind you that the probabilities of more than one god are higher than of one god, because of the math that goes into it. One god would mean one divided by all the other possible outcomes.; that being 2 gods, 3 gods, 4 gods and so on forever. So, basically, infinitely against us. Pure probability seems to state that more than one god is infinitely more probable than one. This is not even taking into account the different variations of a one god existence.

3.12.9 Manipulation

Throughout time, masses have been manipulated by those who controlled belief systems. When money came around those with wealth took control and they merged. The power money buys and fear based religious belief. Money became the dominant force in mental influence. Still, here we are following similar if not the same structures of money and religion. It's time we reform these to serve the species not merely a few. The pyramid scheme works in such a manner that suppresses the majority of people. This is why automation is crucial for the future. In order to advance to the next step of civil evolution we likely should see each individual human as a miracle of creation, and not something we can manipulate from positions of power.

3.12.10 Fallacy of Taking Sides

The major problem with religious belief is the matter of being certain on a side. Humanity has always had one thing in common, the threat of natural disasters. That is what started civilization. Uniting over the fear of being punished by natural disasters. Uniting was key. Today, we have grown apart. The many different religions conflicting, and people using religion to manipulate others into actions that go against the basic concept of unity in the first place. Let's not wait until a natural disaster scares us back into uniting but instead unite together.

Taking a firm position on a single idea of belief systems is flawed, because we do not know what the truth is. We simply know we live, can recreate a conscious, then die. We do know that we are temporary, but the material plane is not. For us to maintain our existence in this material plane, we likely should unite as a race as we have seen proves to lead progress. To unite, we should all agree that we do not know the divine to be a reality, nor can we accurately know if death is the end of our conscious or not. We should take religion for what it is, collections of the most ancient oral traditions we have kept. These stories and beliefs derive from a time when we had no concept of science and rational explanation.

We likely should accept that upon taking religion into our lives, we should use it in a moral sense, not a literal one, since we know the origins of these stories well. Use them to unite and not to divide ourselves. Unfortunately, this is inevitable, and we likely should re-categorize religion as highly improbable theories of afterlife and creation. We should separate the mythological aspects from its moral aspects that best serve survival. God is a mythological concept, but human behavior and morality is not. It is quite real and we experience it every day, so it seems wise to strip all religions of their mythological components and see what you are left with. A set of moral standards.

We see that religion is a framework for the control of populations from the beginning. This belief unified us but now separates us still. Morality is what gave us common ground, which was crucial for pact survival and the transition from hunter-gatherers to farming and agriculture. The major fallacy with believing in a religion is the fact that the probabilities of likely outcomes are infinitely against you. Taking any stance at all would be irrational. Instead accepting we do not know uncertainties is the most rational answer. Accepting that moralities purpose is survival and that it is separate from ideas regarding death and creation.

The real fault is with taking certainty that you know an absolute truth of creation and death. Truth is that the possibilities that exist far outnumber the possibly of anyone one human being correct. The probability will always be infinitely against your idea when taking certainty that you know an answer that is not objectively proven. That is my problem with religion. Seems most logical to be agnostic, but even that can go a couple ways. To simply say I do not know is different than to say there is no way to know. The first is logical while the latter assumes the same fallacy of claiming to know with certainty something that you cannot prove yet or maybe never. This includes atheists. By claiming that they know god does not exist they cling to the fallacy of taking sides. Again, this is basically taking something on faith again.

This does not mean that there is a wealth of moral knowledge and wisdom in looking at our historical religions. I mean, that was how morality was developed. We see that throughout history morality has always led the best survival and growth. Cooperation is better than intimidation; However, the religious fallacy has often best used in the hands of the corrupt to aid violence; something that defies logical morality and is ultimately counterproductive for the species as a unit. We likely should look at religion for what it is; a collection of ancient wisdom based down with roots in oral traditional polytheism. It was a series of treacherous inhumanities suffered by our ancestors that eventually taught us that to survive we likely should unite. Let's not keep paying the same price for the same lesson.

People who still hold onto religious certainties likely should realize that holding a belief that is infinitely improbable is not rational. It has led individuals to commit actions based un uncertainties that originate in oral tradition. Let's come to terms with the fact that we do not know what the truth is about a creator or after life and death. At least not right now we don't, and we may never know for certain. The truth we know, is we die, and we can bring into life a new version of ourselves. This is a much more pleasant way of thinking because it opens up possibilities. From the simple truth that we can create life, we can see that no matter what any religion says, the evidence for physical reincarnation is pretty clear. Any sort of spiritual connection requires more evidence.

4 ECONOMY

"No one should suffer in a world where we print fiat money."

4.1 PERSPECTIVE

Before analyzing economic structures, we should adjust perspectives. Especially, us born in the eighties and beyond, because prior generations come from a different situational landscape. Today, we have access to information that no one else has had before, which makes the general person who is familiar with the internet a lot more informed, or misinformed, than people in the past. For the first time, we have the potential to plainly see societal structures and share this information easily. The lack of communication between the average person was a flaw of old society that dominant forces relied on to maintain coercive control with debt-based dollars.

Current economic structures have roots with coinage and early monotheistic schools of thought around 300 – 500 CE. Growing needs of tracking trade and farming throughout nations created economic systems and writing without future notion of the internet, how big populations would get, and the issues that come with mass energy consumption. Today, with a vastly different technological landscape, we should re-consider the relevance and moral nature of our current economic systems for optimal benefit not for individuals but the species.

It has been a common misconception that the economy is uncontrollable and that government and central banks can only influence the economy in different directions through monetary and fiscal policy. Systems are controllable and appropriate;

therefore, should be dynamic while always improving on themselves. Our monetary system is at the whim of central bankers, when they are the beneficiaries of money supply, when it should be the people. Seems like a re-dressed version of indentured servitude, coated as mortgage and debt when bankers are above its constraints on life; like the old mercantilist view of colonies in which they were merely subordinate producers of wholesaled raw materials for their masters to forge into goods that were sold back to the colonies at premium prices. Okay, so liability sits on general tax payers to work off debt in order to expand the money supply while bankers reap the benefits... these are characteristics of a very self-serving structure that benefits mainly those at the top.

It is possible now with information systems that an economy can be highly controlled and tracked efficiently. The internet and complex information systems are something that have never been around before and works as a fundamental component of unification. For the most efficient possible market to secure the survival of the race and maximize benefit, we should shift from the debt-based fractional reserve lending system of money supply to a needs-based money supply system.

We can all recognize injustice, surely... standards of living have improved in the manner of comfort, given our technology, but not morally and in environmental safety. Most of life's fruit are reaped by the top 10% of the world's people regardless of whether they were the minds behind the progress or the inheritors of luck. Again, a google search will prove that there exists a distortion of wealth distribution; something, that has been true since the beginning of time, when we had no concept of 'logical morality', and now we all believe to have reached such a high level of morality, that we laugh in the face of historical morals. Will not future people be laughing when they look back at our current moral issues? How can it be that the wealth distribution be so much like the primitive times of our past? Is that the kind of legacy we want; 'leave everyone but our fellow countrymen or family, behind?' I *do not* advocate equality of outcome and wealth re-distribution. The innovative spirit should be rewarded and recognized. Individuals who progress and aid the world should be benefit with luxuries, but we should take care of the species; not exploit misfortunes.

What do I mean by exploiting misfortunes? We see it any time one Nation is more technologically or militarily advanced than another. When Europeans came to North America and nearly drove the aboriginal people here extinct by not teaching them to build guns to hold them down with gunpowder supplies. Now they live on small reservations and are hardly taken seriously. We saw it with the original state commissioned pirates. Immorality has been the way of past empires regardless of how they had defined their religious views. "Actions speak louder than words," rings a bell. When Constantine United religion or the Nazi's developed their blitzkrieg. All examples of how nations took advantage of exploits or technology they had. It is time to look to our past and realize the mistakes that were made, learn from them, and create a better future for the species. Not merely those few people born into fortunes, who seem less likely, *not impossible*, to develop genuine morality. I'm not saying that people should not be allowed to accumulate wealth. Of course they should, but let's not leave everyone else at their whim by relying on debt-based money supply systems that are rooted in ancient bank fraud.

4.2 SEPARATION OF NEEDS AND LUXURIES

Most nations have an economic system defined as an arrangement using land, labor, and capital to produce, distribute, and exchange foods and services to meet the needs and wants of people in the society. This definition leaves the *needs* of society at the whim of capitalist markets by combining luxuries and necessities as a single function of our monetary structures. I'm all for free markets for luxury goods. My dispute is that two categories should be implemented; where necessities goods and services industries are run by competing non-profit oriented companies whose reasonable demand becomes the determinant of money supply instead of debt creation by banks. Luxury goods and services markets should solely be free-markets that resemble what we see today, except in the new system there would be no eventual-need for taxes, so markets would experience a new age of liberty. However, no taxation would be a gradual implementation because in the initial transition taxes would be implemented on any luxury product or service as a sales tax. Any money generated from this would simply be deleted as an anti-inflation measure.

Economic structures were established for the greater good, but our economies have evolved over time to serve themselves and those controlling them. For example, the establishment of monopolies, oligopolies, and conglomerates. This has led us into a contrived economic system that boxed us into an individual self-interest-based paradigm, which worked well for us in the past, but should be restructured for modern relevance.

4.3 BORDERS

Borders create an atmosphere of bad competition between groups merely over lines on a map. Divide keeps us from our true potential. Looking to the past, religious schools of thought brought us together and led to our survival and growing standards of living for larger and larger groups. Our differences have led us to separation historically, but we know at a fundamental level, we are strongest united. Benjamin Franklin knew it, the Iroquois knew, all empire builders know it. Drawings, traditions, and superstitions should not divide the species. When we think about ourselves, we think of us as one species, do we not? One unit.

4.3.1   Optimal Resource Usage

The most effective and efficient way to run a single unit such as an intelligent logically moral species is not by separating and competing for scarce resource; but setting, working together to establish optimal use of necessities-based resources for the species survival, as a priority. In an environment with borders, we are forced to produce similar competing commodities in different regions of the world, and not due to geographically physical practicality and efficiency. What does this mean? Let's assume two countries produce two of the same products but each one is proficient at producing the opposite product. On the other hand, each country is better geographically situated for the production of the commodity that they are not proficiently good at producing. Let's assume that this difference evens out their production capacities. Logic dictates that each country switch labor and focus solely on what they are proficient than trade with its neighbor. This would increase total production output if looking at them in aggregate, or single unit.

If they compete, they are less likely to share trade secrets that make them proficient. If we withhold information, the unit as a whole produces less output. Borders are hindering in this sense of lowering overall lower production levels of a single unit such as the human species. Civilizations form by uniting people. However, many united people were done under force which is not sustainable. Ultimately, there is great global production benefit if all countries allow for the free immigration of populations, the sharing of experience, knowledge, and combing the species needs production. This unity would allow for all proficient people to focus on their areas of expertise. It would also greatly lesson the need of transportation of goods because the best routes could be established without political drama.

Conclusively, a society without borders would allow for the optimal allocation of earth's geography and natural resource for a needs-based money supply system to work efficiently. Open trade agreements between nations are a small step toward this idea of no borders but do not scratch the surface. The European trade union being an even bigger step. However, it uses the old monetary system of fractional reserve banking which will consistently fail to provide the best benefit available to the species. A needs-based money supply system is required for this pivotal transition period.

4.3.2   Perpetual Power Struggle

Borders manifest a perpetual struggle between nations for foreign trade power. Forever nations will exert their economic power over others. By getting rid of borders, there is no upper hand to be had on anyone else because we are united. Modern economic systems develop bordered nations to compete on who can produce the most GDP when in reality maximum production levels cannot be achieved with such a centralized self-serving structure that leaves masses of living beings unappropriated, neglected, and suffering around the world. All societal structures inherited from the actions and traditions of our ancestors. They established what we live in; yet, we laugh at their misunderstandings of logical morality.

What are the possible outcomes of such a system that border themselves from one another? One all powerful nation that economically cripples the others? A single nation that holds so much military power and influence that they suppress everyone else into a lower class that labors away at all the undesirable duties that come with modern society? What is the range of possible outcomes of a species with borders as we have them today? What are the possibilities of a species without borders? Think about it yourself. The outcomes of borders will always suffer the consequences of a divided species, while open-borders leads to integration and synergy. Ultimately, we likely should accept one another into our lives and see past our differences, because when it comes to life and death, we are all here for the same ride. If there is only one team, there can only be one winner of survival. If there are many nations competing there will always be conflict and many will suffer at the benefit of one.

What is the consequence of every nation doing only what is best for themselves, at the cost of the rest of the world; because, *that,* is what we have in the world. It will always be resentment and spitefulness toward that country by the others who are consider beneath them. It's this air of superiority nations embrace that creates the conflict. Instead of us all saying okay let's get rid of this idea of borders... let's travel and trade freely without interference... let's combine essentials industries, we argue and impose ideas on others that suit our needs over theirs. This structure will always be a perpetual power struggle.

4.3.3   Separation of Borders and Traditions

A major significance we tend to give borders are cultural traditions of people within those borders. Borders and traditions are separate. Because traditions derive from ancient beliefs, traditions become less and less relevant as time goes on, but borders stay the same. Any idea that without borders traditions would disappear is irrational. Borders are simply bureaucratic systems of inefficiency and is a separate concept from cultural traditions.

Traditions are mostly bad when they hold people in past ways of doing things for the mere reason that it is the past way of doing things. A logical fallacy; especially, if a better way exists. Taking that into consideration all traditions should be reconsidered. Traditions should be malleable and be thrown out when need be. Holding on to date traditions might provide nostalgia, but it is simply a past habit.

4.3.4   World Without Borders

Imagine you could travel and work anywhere without a Visa. All your needs including education and basic food and shelter would be met anywhere you want to go. Imagine you are a citizen of the world and everywhere you went within the Global Union, you could get any essential of living for free. A single passport of humanity that never expires allowing you to work and travel within the union. That is what the world should be. Why is it not that way? What would it take? A single act that is not based on a nations self-interest?

We should stop separating ourselves. It doesn't matter what language you speak, gender, or skin tone, we are all the same organization. The human-being. That is what we are first and above all. We all share the same birth and we all share the pain of death, loss, suffering, joy, and happiness in our lives. All the fundamentals. We all know these. Why separate ourselves with drawings? We can keep our culture's and differences. Borders tie back to the need to feel superior and the greedy-accumulation of scarce resource.

Getting rid of borders is the first step toward uniting the world. Our politicians and leader's efforts should be focused on making these things happen if we want to reach our ultimate potential. With the help of a needs-based money supply system and open border policies that combine nations essentials markets, humanity can take initial steps toward a Global Union. We, *the people*, who need to push for these things to occur, because politicians are mostly in it for themselves. We should take it to the good ones and show them there is a better way. First, we should let go of our traditional ties to the past and move forward as a single race that cares for one another.

How would the world look with equal opportunity and love for the species? Ask yourself if that's a world you want to live in. I'm not saying communism. That has proven not to work, but the fact that we have not come up with more ideas and systems for the world is astonishing; this should be a never-ending pursuit of perfecting ourselves for our specie's longest possible survival.

4.3.4.1   Separation of Borders and Currency

At first, nations could simply get rid of border guards and patrol without combining currencies. No natural rule says we must open borders and at the same time combine currencies. That is a contrived paradigm. What is the point of separating identities through nationalities when we're all citizens of the world? Removal of citizenship requirements for jobs in nations such as the Europeans have done makes the most sense. Imagine, like dominos, countries allow for open immigration and removal of customs. Airport protection should still be in place and increased with out of work border guards. These nations would combine their essentials-based industries for money supply as borders open. They could still have their own currencies, and all currencies would be accepted through the union at first to ease transition.

4.3.4.2 *Ultimate peace*

The use of borders is a leading cause of war and tension. Patriotism should evolve to include the entire human species. A world without borders would ultimately lead to world peace because people would stop seeing themselves as different. By living as neighbors, they could have the chance to realize that we all have something in common… *love*. Open borders coupled with a needs-based money supply system is an essential step in the evolution of our collective subconscious, that will finally abolish racism and discrimination. Nothing will exist to physically separate us again; unless we let it.

4.3.4.3 *Narcotics Trade*

Some will argue that open borders would allow illegal narcotics to flourish, but the solution for that is simple. Legalize all use for adults after a legal age and take control of the production and distribution within the luxuries market. Allow for no black markets to exist, as they only lead to violence and crime. Instead develop markets around them and enlighten your people, in the classical sense.

Just to show some logic of this benefit is the quality control of narcotics. The unfortunate reality is that by keeping it illegal, we lower the quality of the drugs, which keeps margins very high for criminals. The other unfortunate reality is that supply is nearly unlimited anywhere you go. In every large city I have been to, if you walk the downtown streets looking, you will find the drug spots. So how effective is this war on drugs? It could easily be construed, at this point, to be a complete inside job by corrupt officials. Either it's an inside job or borders are completely inefficient in stopping the traffic of narcotics, which means they are just a hassle for average travelers. Any hassles of this nature are counterproductive for unit production output. It is safe to say that full control of narcotics has never existed; instead, the enormous markets that exist for it have always maintained a supply. By keeping it illegal, we simply increase violence, criminal profit margins, and lowers quality.

4.3.4.4 *Extra resource*

Anyone misplaced from work that could not find new work could simply return to school for free education in a needs-based money supply system. Incentivizing misplaced workers to establish bio-friendly automation to sustain the world's necessities markets production would be set as a priority until achieved. No one wants to work tedious horrible jobs. The government's priority should be achieving freedom for the people if they truly have their best interest in mind, which would free us to follow our passions. Not only that, it is the only way humans can properly allocate the time needed to proactively enhance human evolution, which I believe will yield an unprecedented level of heightened human ingenuity.

4.3.4.5 *European Union*

Europe started the transition. At this point they should establish a needs-based monetary system as described in the conclusion section of this chapter. To continue their directive, they should attempt to persuade additional nations to open borders with Europe under a needs-based monetary system. A good start would be Brazil. I would recommend the United States do it, but given the president currently in place, I doubt it would fly. They do not need to combine currencies if so desired, as we have seen the issues that accompanies such actions. Merely the abolishment of borders without currency unification will accommodate a transition to unite the world. Eventually, when majority of borders have opened, the union of currencies would seem much more reasonable and likely. All currencies would be accepted in places of business within the union and the open market would naturally play its process. If desired, private central banks could still operate within this new money supply system. Hardly anything changes at first. It is a gradual progression consisting of micro steps followed by analysis and revisions that starts with multiple nations letters of intent to join the Global Union. The agreement must combine needs-based markets which would be the determinant of new money supply.

4.4 GDP Run Economy

With an economy based on gross domestic product, governments constantly try to figure out new production. This is counterproductive though; regardless of how counter intuitive it sounds at first, because we create so many means of production, such as expiration of a passport and fees, only so our country produces more GDP. Being that every service or payment that is made contributes to GDP, this creates an incentive to over bureaucratize and over penalize people over the mere attempt of generating higher GDP and tax income. So, what at first appears to be productive in the way of creating tedious bureaucracy and services taxpayers are forced to use, is anti-progressive and anti-productive.

It also allows for major corporations and money to influence politics because companies are the largest producers of GDP. The problem with this model is that governments start looking at tax payers as a means to an end instead of being real living people with families that have lives with accompanying worries and problems. Taxation creates a government view that resembles a greedy corporation.

4.4.1   Corporate Government

Governments are run like enterprises in the twenty first century. Corporations are run based on self-interest and self-growth and preservation in a competitive landscape. This view is not one that seems appropriate for that of running a species of intelligent logically moral beings. For the purposes of economy, we see how the corporate view of government contains the self-interest aspects of a corporation. For example, the hierarchical structure of leadership. The shareholders in turn would be the corporations that invest in the politicians that get elected, while the customer is the tax payer or consumer of the service sold by the government corporation.

The government is no more than a monopolized services corporation that has convinced its clients, to give them full authority and creation power of their laws to elected psychological manipulators. They don't print the money or control the money supply. Government is in charge of legislation and social services. A government should not be a company who sells services. Instead it is meant to represent the needs of people. Today they are mostly run as corporations serving their investors at the expense of the tax payers. The entire thing needs to be reformed, but further discussions on this is reserved for the government chapter.

4.5 MONETARY SYSTEM

4.5.1 Money and Division

Some people only want to get by while others seek to maximize the amounts they make in their single life time. Regardless, money is the number one controller of an average person's life. This is due to the fact that money rules the necessities of living; like health care, food, dwelling, water, education, public safety, and energy among others. Money is the major cause of stress in people's lives. Stress is not only a leading indicator of bad health, but quality of life as well. For example, couples often break up over differences on money. Mostly we are tied into the monetary system unless we live out in the few tribal societies that exist today; therefore, is one of the major components of mass population control.

It has become so bad, that money controls us and our actions rather than we control money and how we define money. This has allowed for small groups of individuals who stumbled upon its influence over the masses. Money is simply a measurement device for trade. However, we see the obvious misappropriation of this money with the Hollywood film 'Alpha Dog,' which was based on a true story. People use money to measure up against each other and feel superior so they can distinct themselves from everyone else. Money pins us against each other while we should stick together, which ultimately leads to war and self-destruction as with borders. Money in the form that we see it today should only govern the luxuries market. The necessities market as previously mentioned requires a readjusted system.

Any society that creates tension and separation such that money and borders create will never evolve into its true potential for production and efficiency as a single unit. Our perception of money needs to change. Money Supply exists to serve the public, not banking individuals, and that should be the view. Fractional reserve banking seems not to follow this principle. Any goods and services classified as a human need will operate differently than luxury markets. This does not mean that there cannot be different outfits and competition for needs, but they would be funded differently. All Global Union members would have rights to essentials goods and services classified as needs, so that the stresses of survival can be eliminated for all global citizens. This sounds like a huge change and it is… no doubt. However, just because a change is big does not mean it should not be done.

4.5.2 Federal Reserve

It is a private bank owned by member banks. However, it has a shady history being named 'federal' reserve to mislead the public. Why else would it have Federal in that name, while remaining private? Federal reserve board members determine what average taxpayer's debt payments are going to be and whether they have a job or not, which gives the fed extraordinary influence over the American population' standard of living. Not saying to take the fed down or get rid of a central bank concept, I agree that we need that kind of institution. It is fractional the reserve banking model that I find out dated. No need to kill me, I believe all nations within my model should indeed keep their own central banks; therefore, keeping all current financial infrastructures in place.

4.5.2.1 *Fed 4-step Money Making Process in a nutshell.*

1. Federal Open Market Committee Approves purchase of U.S Bonds.

2. The Fed purchases bonds.

3. Fed pays for the bonds with <u>baseless</u> electronic credits to the seller's banks accounts.

4.   Banks use these deposits as reserves. They can loan out a lot more than their reserves to new borrowers; at interest, which creates new money but only in the form of debt.

4.5.2.2 *Fractional reserve banking. "Debt Servitude"*

Why is money creation held from the people by banks using a derivative form of defrauding the public? Bankers first discovered this method of banking centuries ago. We cannot exactly date it, because it was likely kept a secret from the public by the bankers who practiced this. At some point in history, Bankers discovered they could loan more money than they had in their holdings, because they hardly ever had account withdrawals. This in turn would have created more money in society.

4.5.2.3 *Simple Hypothetical Examples*

Say there was 1,000,000 dollars in a bank. That banker loans out 2,000,000 for a cost of 100,000. This practice creates the bank 1,000,000 dollars profit out of thin air that the borrower has to pay back and never existed in the first place plus 100,000. Whenever they got too greedy there would be hyperinflation. Luckily for currency creators, likely broke these loans down at first and with population growth aiding their scheme, they got away for a long time. How does population growth help this plan?

Think about it like this… there are 10,000 people in a society and 100,000 gold coins to go around. (100,000/10,000=10 per person.) If next year there are 20,000 people but still 100,000 to go around. There is a problem; less money to go around. (100,000/20,000=5 per person.) Especially, if commerce for needs and luxury goods are combined, because merchants naturally accumulate wealth and save it. This natural inclination further contributes to the lessening of money supply for those 20,000 people.

If out of that 100,000, a currency creator creates new gold coins with less gold and loans out 10,000 extra coins from this process; they add 10,000 to the original 100,000. We have the original from of fractional reserve system. So, at the end of year one, when there were 20,000 people, there would be 110,000 coins for the market. This is a very simple example of how the fractional reserves system concept originated in early societies… fractional reserve banking is no fundamentally different than debasing gold coins. Empires would grow their economies themselves adding economic expansion through war and mining, which further aided these currency creation schemes that evolved into societal structures. Back then, no one kept track of the empire's entire money supply, and if they tried, it would have been difficult. Gold base was the favorite base for coinage because it was impossible to counterfeit.

This example shows the power and influence that is given to the money creators, nowadays, central banks. It also shows that economic expansion heavily links with population size is actually a good thing for growing populations. However, in fractional reserves banking, central banks are the gatekeepers of money by holding the public economically at their mercy. Expanding the money supply requires the public to borrow money from banks at interest. If populations increase and money does not, the accumulating traits of commerce will slowly run the system dry. Bankers and politicians are easily able to get away with this practice under veil of complexity.

The current market system naturally dries the money up through pyramid schemes that serve few at the top and the immediate wealth classes below them. They will tell you that they lend it back out to the society, but that is the whole scheme to begin with. Keep as many people as possible in debt servitude. From the practical a-moral perspective of keeping labor growing, it works, yet, not the definition of liberty. It is merely a structured redefinition of old fashioned coercive power structures that had slaves and indentured servitude, which does not follow the spirit of every human being born equal by natural law. Money creation should not be held hostage in exchange for debt, which is psychologically damaging and forces people into jobs they protect over automation when automation should be classified as a human necessity. Human beings are being robbed of their precious time in this existence that is nothing less than a miracle, on top of missing out on proactively enhancing our species evolution for maximum benefit and capacity.

It's 2018 and I live in a Constitutional Monarchy, that still has its money supply produced by something labeled the 'Royal Canadian Mint' and the Central Bank of Canada governs Monetary and Fiscal Policy. As famously quoted, "let us control the money of a nation, and we care not who makes its laws" was known to be a "maxim" of the House of Rothschilds. Quotes such as these are only true if essentials and luxuries markets are combined and we continue to use the fractional reserve banking system that indebts the public to expand the economy.

Money supply should be linked to the needs of the people and is the purpose of my needs-based dollar. Instead, today the money supply system relies on good people having dreams of owning a home and indebting themselves to create money that will always end up in the hands of the few accumulators at the top of a pinnacle system. People who are immune to real-estate bubbles and interest rate hikes. Debt comes with severe psychological damage, which I feel in my own life and seen others suffer even worse, like my friend who has struggled with ten-thousand-dollar credit card debts for almost ten years now and feels like an interest worker. Yet, his pride won't allow him to declare bankruptcy. Shows the type of psychological damage it does.

In conclusion the payment of bank loans creates money in the fractional reserve system, which in slowly ends up with the top few who put that new money back out in the form of loans lowering interest rates further. In the sense of keeping average people perpetually working, it works, but it does so at mass psychological damage and the expense of evolution. Additionally, it shifts responsibility of overall survival away from societies elected leaders, who are chosen for this purpose. Banks create loans for the average person to work off based on nothing while elect leaders get to play popularity contests and flip-flop on legislation to unrepresented masses.

We established societal structures for a 'dog eat dog world,' when it could be unified. From the banker's perspective, it's glorious, because this system creates classes of debt servitude, where bankers run supreme. And what better motivation for borrowers than losing their dreams of the freedom those with wealth have? Fractional reserve banking started out as fraud and displays the moral nature of those who advocate such a system. Yet, it has become the official way in which money is created around the world. Every citizen should be familiar with the money supply they live in. Money is an underlying component within society that affects everyone whether we like it or not.

4.5.2.4 Low Interest Rates

Why are interest rates so low? Likely, because of hoarded money that is filtered to the top few who will always be lenders. That is not to say they are bad, because there are many good people with money. Having money or being a banker does not make someone bad when they are born into a highly, if not fully, deterministic system to begin with. However, they should also understand that there is always a better way to reach a more efficient and logically moral society.

4.5.2.5 Replacement of the Fractional Reserve Banking

A need for a new money supply system has emerged with the advent of automation and robotics. My needs-based money supply system allows for the creation of money to come through the production of needs-based products and services instead of debt. A needs-based money supply system will create abundance, accurate statistical data, and controlled expansion of the money supply. Analysts at central banks would monitor inflation and play stabilizing roles to avoid hyperinflation. This transition would be an ongoing development, which would effectively boost innovation in all needs-based goods and services industries. The nature of such a system would be dynamic as to easily adapt to new relevancies.

4.6 FINAL WORDS ON ECONOMY

The ideal Economy wouldn't leave anyone behind by taking logical morality into consideration. It would make the species survival a priority; yet, still provide a free market that allows us to earn luxuries by pursuing our dreams and creating benefits for society. A needs-based economy would bolster innovation in all industries and free people of the stresses that largely create violence and crime in society. The first steps require us to open our minds to breaking away from the separation of ourselves with borders that contrive our idea of what a society is; that being not national, but global.

4.6.1 Capitalism – Global Dream

The capitalist manifesto is financial freedom. Being able to live life without working medial jobs for hourly wages. Isn't that what everyone wants? To have the freedom to pursue our dreams? Think about the potential that goes to waste every year, because the masses do not have the financial freedom to pursue what we truly desire. It's the current world's biggest waste of human resource, talent, and natural evolution regardless of all the great things it has accomplished. So much of today's success attributes to luck or circumstance, which makes true capitalism difficult to achieve. The separation of needs and luxuries markets is required if we are all to have the benefits that accompanies financial freedom. Every human should have those benefits with regards to their survival needs for a healthy standard of living. By facilitating a Global Union of citizens with freedom and evolved environments, we will produce, innovate, and evolve at accelerated rates. General health and longevity would increase and technology will reach higher levels.

4.6.2   Needs-Base Money Supply System

The first major need would be automation, which would best benefit the species, since it will literally replace people's means to survive. The very people which have enriched all those who have managed to achieve financial freedom. One hundred percent automation is the next phase of mechanical evolution which allows us to shift our focus toward a new society.

What does it mean to be categorized as a necessity under this money supply system? These goods and services are exempt from the stresses of failure given they have a provable demand. That demand would be tracked to determine the amount of new money that is created in the form of company expenses. Expenses would be for the cost of the publics usage up to their maximum periodic limits which would not include a markup, but rather, the real-time market price for the good based on supply and demand.

Accounting systems would record and track all expenses that companies require to operate most efficiently; then a publicly elected authority in charge of money supply, such as the federal reserve, would bring the funds required for their operating expenses into existence. In the beginning of such a system transition careful analysis must be put into which industries in addition to automation would convert first to a necessities classification in order to avoid hyperinflation. However, health, law enforcement, and food should be among the first considered along with automation.

A benchmark number would be used from previous years of money supply expansion to be compared and matched with aggregate expenses for different top essentials outfits, prioritized by market share, to convert as needs first to maintain inflation stability. Government run industries expenses would be assessed on aggregate. The established benchmark would be the periodic cap of money creation that can be created with stable inflation. It could also be adjusted on a monthly, quarterly, or annual basis for relevance to population numbers or the ratio of per capita wealth.

To reiterate, the benchmark number would be the chosen period amount of new money created with loans in form of fractional reserve banking. This expansion number should correlate with global population of the union on a variable base. Various multiples can be tested once an operational system is implemented, but this does not have to be so. Because of the pyramid money accumulation model already in place, those at the top of luxuries markets, would greatly benefit from the new model. It's honestly an all-around win for the species; increases the whole pie. Banks in this system would be left with only lending what they have policy which would in turn drive up interest rates for their loans which should boost their business since getting loans for luxury-based business ideas would be a business entitled to them and private equity firms only.

Markets that are classified as an essential would operate in the same competitive nature as they do now; only difference being they would be the determinant of money creation. Because a good or service provided by a needs company is offered to the citizen at a fairly established price given supply and demand, every citizen is credited a periodic dollar value amount only usable on needs-based goods and services that is appropriately determined for their healthy survival. This periodic amount would best be done on a daily basis for food and would not accumulate or could accumulate with a diminishing return. The point of this is that if a person doesn't require that product or service that day, it is more efficient to not accumulate because it was not a requirement of survival as per judgement of the person. Any purchases made above the daily credit amount would cost regular funds already under circulation and carry a premium. Because this kind of revenue would be pure profit in a needs-based business that has expenses covered by money creation, it would act as a counter measure to lessen the need for money creation by replacing it dollar for dollar; this could also be a variable conversion based on anti-inflation needs. So, for every dollar that comes in above a person's daily allowable amount required for healthy survival, a dollar less is required of the money supply system. By doing this, freedom is still available for those with more wealth, while the essentials for a healthy survival will be covered for all Global-Union citizens.

This model would guarantee the survival of all needs-based industries. It is crucial that money creation only benefit companies with provable market bases, which keeps competition alive within businesses. A redrafted competition act would be required for the needs industry. Needs-based businesses will not have shareholders, only initial founders, staff, and management if required, which will give them no self-interest bias; with a goal to automate everything eventually. Essentials companies' existences will still only be determined by the amount of people using their services. Payment for salaries and royalties of such companies would be printed into existence and deposited into the appropriate individual's account. Founders would have the choice of continuing in business activities or being paid a set passive royalty after the business has been automated or has been newly converted. Previous shareholders of newly converted firms would have flexible options of continued royalty payments or fair value buyout at conversion. Any royalties paid to founders would continue, given the business serves the public interest and would have a direct link to the firm's demand; this means they would continue past the founder's life.

The needs of people within the combined nations that absolve their borders would be measured by information systems that give people reasonable dollar credit limits to use essential goods and services as they require them for survival. Different industries would have different periodic durations. Something like food would be on a daily, weekly, or even optional basis while medical and dental would have an unlimited amount for reasonable healthy survival needs. Doctors, dentists, and researchers in these fields would have the unlimited backing of money creation to support any plausible research projects and reasonable salaries given benefits to society are proven. Some credits would accumulate while others wouldn't. These aspects would be determined on trial basis as we gain experience with such a monetary system. A universal information system would track the usage of all needs-based goods and services to create population statistics instead of samples.

Ultimately, we would have a system where money is created as needs-based goods and services are provided for the species survival instead of debt. Citizens can use these monies to spend on the existing luxuries market and it will fuel the constant circulation and velocity of money. So, when a citizen requires one of these necessities, they go in to use the service and pay nothing up to their allowed credit dollar value. This means it would never cost anything for the reasonable necessities of life. How alleviating would that be? We can all agree that we need these to survive and the world was naturally inherited by the entire species not merely a few of us with circumstantial luck. On the other hand, if you wanted luxuries in your life, you would have to earn it. Also, if machines do our physical labor we are left to naturally evolve ourselves into our most evolved selves biologically.

This needs-based system would foster innovation by making it possible for any new entrepreneur to build a business plan and submit it to an agency that would decide funding based on their professionalism, credentials, and viability to produce benefits for the species. Innovation would be money creation, so a major incentive for progress. Oppositely in the luxuries market there would be an increased inflow of capital leading to surpluses of venture capital for luxury markets investing. Payment of the union's essentials markets would be made under equivalent-value conversion rates no matter what currency to the receiver.

*The following list of industries should ultimately be classified as needs in a perfect world, but it is likely that only a select number will be viable at first to avoid hyperinflation and problems due to rapid changes in market dynamics.

4.6.2.1   *Ultimately all the necessities to be competing essentials-based corporations*

- Agriculture
- Automation
    - o   Artificial Intelligence
    - o   Robotics
    - o   Information Systems for Accounting and statistical information building.
- Basic Medical Services
- Cattle Ranchers/Livestock
    - o   Meat Processing
- Chemical and Related Manufacturing
- Crop Production and Basic Processing
- Residential Construction
- Defense Weapons Research and Manufacturing
- Education
- Energy and Natural Resource

- News Dissemination

- Property Ownership

- Research (Anything)
    - Biological
    - Environment Sustainability
    - Evolutionary
    - Longevity

- Law Enforcement

- Fire Safety

- Commodity Transportation

- Needs-based Pharmaceuticals

- Power and Utilities

- Real Estate

- Public Transit

- Grocery Retailers

- Residential Construction

- Garbage disposal and recycling

The first things to go essentials should be automation, health services and food production. Everything else would convert in due time. This following list is simply an example and may contain additional items. The ultimate determinant would be inflation stability.

4.6.3   Anti-Inflation

With automation as an essential technology. Any luxuries companies would pay a variable fee for the use of these technologies as a dollar for dollar anti-inflation measure; this conversion rate could be variable and linked with anti-inflation needs. During the transition we should hold sales tax on all luxury transactions as anti-inflation measure. Tax would be used as an anti-inflation tool during the transition, but when this new society has fully formed, which may take generations, tax would be weeded out completely.

4.6.4 Land/Property rights

This is tough to admit, because I always planned to one day retire off rental property. The reality is that rental properties in the manner that we see them used today qualifies as abuse. Rental properties split people up between land owners and renters, which creates division. A concept such as no rental properties may be hard to accept but would fit a needs-based money supply system. Short-term rentals such as hotels, bnbs, and shared accommodations would still be allowed. Short-term rentals would be encouraged and partly incentivized by money supply given inflation plausibility.

It is in the spirit of adjusting morality within large apartment rental conglomerates that secure countless small spaces under long-term rental contracts, that I say this. This idea will likely come under heavy scrutiny and does not need be implemented if collective morality has not yet reached this point. However, I urge society to look at the events with mortgages in 2008 and understand that shelter is a human need that everyone deserves without having to contract their earnings to landlords. A limit on property ownership is right, which comes from logical reasoning on a basis of morality and best benefit for the species. Limits should range from four to seven homes per person; that means eight to fourteen for married couples. Size and acreage should not have limits. However, all usable farmlands must be farmed in such a system.

My work in this book assumes four residential homes per individual and eight for married couples. Rich people with the maximum number of homes could offer short-term rentals and still earn passive income that is incentivized by the monetary system to the inflation stability cap. There are many directions in which the rules on property could go, but for a genuine needs-based dollar to hold the best benefits for the species survival, rental laws should be reconsidered.

4.6.4.1 Incentivized short-term rentals

What this means is that everyone who does not yet own four properties would have an annual dollar credit for travel accommodations, which will be created by the needs-based money supply system. This would be influenced by the benchmark periodic cap. Surpluses would add to these funds. It could also be taken for expenditures over the basic amounts. These special accumulating accounts will be restricted to vacation accommodations usage, which in turn end up getting spent on short-term rentals.

4.6.4.2 *Limit Extension*

A bypass on the ownership limit could be created in the form of making ownership of houses above the limit come with an annual fee in the form of money already in circulation. That would be the only thing resembling a tax in society. The reason for this is to limit the inefficiencies that come with hoarding of a scarce assets such as property.

4.6.4.3 *Protect Our Children*

One possible eventual structure, meaning not instant, to consider follows; every family consisting of a married couple, defined as two life partners of any sex who plan to raise children, or single parent with child is able to raise the child or children while living in a vacant home of their choosing rent-free for the benefit of evolution. During the time of raising children, the money supply system would increase the parent's basic periodic limits.

Any citizen above a legal adult age will be given the choice to live with their parents or relocate to a vacant single's home of their choosing. Parents would be additionally compensated for raising children in the best proactive evolutionary manner available by research institutions. Children would also be compensated for their discipline in naturally enhancing evolution. It's a difficult job but evolution is our future. To allow liberty, families are allowed to forego the extra incentives and lead any evolutionary life style they desire. However, their base-periodic-dollar-credits would be survival-needs only; putting more pressure on them to find work if they require luxury goods and services.

4.6.4.4 *No Value Lost*

My way of thought here will likely be met with strong counter arguments because of the controversy that it encompasses. The idea that people cannot own rental properties. Let that sink in...

but what does it mean? At first, a market value would be assessed for currently owned rental properties in which the owners are fairly compensated for their assets. No value would be lost, instead it would be gained, because the needs markets would cover their essentials, so their money would have greater purchasing power within the luxury markets. Land owners with more than the voted-on limit on personal residential property ownership at initial system transition would be ranked by total asset values, and they would be given choice at their four primary homes. They can always purchase new homes in exchange for their four primary homes, but there is no point in hording hundreds or thousands of rental properties. Let me emphasize that in such a system no property taxes on a person's first four homes would exist. Eight for couples.

Deemed sales of rental property would be considered sold to the monetary system first than immediately to the current renters at zero interest, who would have flexible repayments of the fair value of their properties toward ownership. The initial fair values will be credited to the previous owners while the renter's repayments would counter act dollar for dollar future money supply during the transition process. Initial conversions would give landowners with too many properties enormous sums of money that would provide endless lives of extravagance for them and their future generations. Most of which will be kept safe in conservative interest-bearing accounts. Nothing would change other than there would be no rental properties, nor vacant properties. Real estate bubbles would be a thing of the past; therefore, lowering suffering for the species.

The richest who have more than four private homes during initial transition will choose their four primary homes, and if they chose not to deem sales, they will be charged property tax or allow the reassigned of the extra homes to anyone of their choosing that is of age. The value of their surplus homes would be compensated to the owners in the form of future credits that would grow at interest but be restricted to be periodically dispensed in congruence with inflation stability. Anyone who does not currently own a house or rent one would choose on a first come first serve basis one primary vacant apartment to be their home in which they have to pay a monthly mortgage that would eventually become their first homes. Mortgages will always be set as a percent of income for all adults. This means that any person coming of age will be allowed a free first mortgage on a home if they can't afford one. For current renters, all that would change would be their rental agreements. Rent payments would convert into mortgage payments. This deal can only be arranged on first homes. Anything beyond your first should be acquired through the regular banking system or accumulated savings.

4.6.4.4.1 New Home Incentive Program

Building better replacement homes for those who have accomplished owning four houses would be incentivized with inflation stable annual money creation limits that are systematically awarded by lottery to anyone who owns four homes. Anyone can forego this lottery benefit and gain instead a reasonable passive income in return. This serves to balance further losses from rental rights. Because residential construction becomes a necessity and new property construction will be needed to match vacant homes to populations, this market would boom. It would also make it easier for society to remodel our transportation infrastructures. By making owning four homes an incentive people will strive to produce benefits for society in order to improve the luxuries in their lives.

4.6.4.5 *Single's Without Short-Term Goals of Raising Children*

This question should be answered when we are at the age of adulthood. At an early age we should be aware of the different paths these decisions will have on our lives. However, this does not mean that people can't change their minds. Not at all, but those who initially decide to wait would be allocated to an apartment until they want to raise a family. Couples with families will be given priority over multi-room homes. Single people could earn themselves enough to buy whatever-size home they desire. Singles who are wealthy can also purchase any four homes they desire at adulthood. This is an idea for consideration that I believe would likely yield significant removal of stress that would in turn enhance not only evolution, but global conflict. Perfecting this model would take trial and error but would greatly aid natural evolution and survival of the species.

4.6.4.6 *Effect on Construction*

Doing this would bolster construction, because it becomes a necessity for people to reach the capacity of homes that correlates with population. This sort of system allows for the proper organization of new residential developments and would increase economic expansion. Proper construction projects with the people's benefit in mind would be the ones that got approved. Transportation could be restructured for efficiency and effectiveness.

4.6.4.7 *Transition*

For smoother transition a large coalition of nations must sign letters of intent to open borders and combine needs market money supply systems before implementation to effectively correlate plans for the change. Committees of specialists would combine all laws and classifications for initial transition. Like I commented before, Europe is best situated for this and likely would do well by combining with Brazil, which would reinforce economic independence of such a union. Nations that do not enter the agreement, which would hold an open invitation, will be completely barred from trade with the union until they abolish debt-based money supply systems and open their borders. This will lead the entire world into a borderless world of abundance that serves the entire species. The technology for unity is at our feet, all we need to do is implement.

4.6.5 Automation

Automation and robotics is the primary need for humanity. We require near full automation to free the masses from tedious physical labor that hinders brain evolution. The truth is we're slacking when it comes to evolving our brains. We hardly use them and we avoid putting them through logic testing, puzzles, meditation, and visualizations. Things that are necessary to healthy brain evolution. When we have a world that is completely automatic, we will have to work extra hard to keep active brains or else we will risk devolving into continually smaller brains. Automation is therefore the most important human need today, but also the biggest threat to our existence. Not by forceful take over, but by devolving our brains because life is too easy. Implementing automation means we have increased responsibility to our physical and mental health.

Because automation and robotics becomes a human need, we would eventually reach a point where tedious physical labor is a thing of the past. Today people are afraid of losing their trucking jobs which represent a large portion of North American jobs. Self-driving trucks are coming out and all these people will be out of work. Well this needs-based-money supply system fixes that, because it covers their basic needs and makes free re-education an available transition option. Including their homes. Anyone who can prove they reasonably cannot find work and are out of employment due to automation, but do not yet own a single home will have the money supply system cover their payments as a means of money creation. This amount will be determined by inflation stability conversion rates.

4.6.6 Food production

Another primary concern should be the health and quality of what we eat. In a profit-oriented industry that places food production alongside luxuries markets, we allow it to fall to the corrupting influence of greed created by the accumulation of money. Thus, we see unethical farming of animals and high rates of low quality cancerous food products. A needs-based money supply system would create an unbiased group of educated professionals, funded by money creation, that are dedicated to understanding the best forms of food production and nutrition for us and nature. Prices would be set to appropriate supply and demand for products. Ethical farming practices could be reintroduced and prices would fluctuate while other means of meat production like hunting may surge. Also, there may be a bigger incentive for smaller farms and farmer communities to develop instead of large factory farms. I'm definitely not saying ban meat farming, but let's make it ethical and let supply and demand determine the price.

4.6.6.1 *Factory Farming*

We should stop unethically factory farming animals... this does not mean vegetarianism. It just means ethical moral farming of animals by increased farm sizes and agriculture. Do we really think of ourselves as a race who will captivate an animal and pump them full of hormones without living a single day in natural sunlight before they are slaughtered?

Agricultural automation should be highly incentivized and prioritized under a needs-based money supply system to reach a point where farming is not laborious for humans, but rather we could live in the country side leisurely overlooking the automation process of farming that is done in ethical manner; something like solar. This is a transitionary process that could take a long time but would benefit our society. It would also create incentives for hunting and likely creating a hunter's meat market, which could become highly profitable as adjusted initial lower supply would likely drive prices up. Yet, the urge is strong and well ingrained in our culture to factory farm.

I find it likely that by turning our heads to factory farming, we disconnect further from nature and morality. Because we are willing to turn our heads to unethical practices of animal farming, that the habit might indirectly influence us to turn our heads to other immoral things, which can become a slippery slope. We likely should look at our collective actions and consider that these actions may have a more profound effect on our psychology than appears at first.

All societal structures have authority ranked into a pyramid structure, which likely sips into our psychology and forms the way people use our natural resources including animals. I am not against hunting; in fact, hunting is the purest natural form of meat farming we could practice. Hunting should be regulated to be an enduring sport. A higher market price of meat would drive the hunting business up as people who want meat would likely take to hunting or take to community farming where they can raise their animals ethically.

There are areas of the wilderness where hunting is required and thus would help nature while supporting ethical animal farming. Because farming and meat production would become an essentials-based industry eventually, this activity would also be incentivized by money supply. No companies would be forced out of business. Instead owners would be either compensated in purchase form or hold a right to royalties based on use of their land or previous business. All without direct responsibilities if they so desired. The goal would be to keep the previous owners at the same level of benefit or better than they would have been before the needs-based money supply system. Not only would owners be compensated for having run an essentials-based business, there would be great flexibility in their options.

4.6.7 Environment

Nature and the environment are the most important things to consider when innovating. Working together with nature, we likely should create ways to enhance our ecological systems. By allowing the research and sustainability of the environment to be a source of money supply, we will see our knowledge in this field flourish. Terra forming earth itself would become incentivized, which may lead to completely new discoveries. In fact, we will see all necessity categorized industries thrive because anyone with a viable project that will benefit society will ultimately be funded.

4.6.8 Wealth Distribution

Wealth distribution is something that will never work because humans are unique; therefore, some work harder than others. In my needs-based system, this will stay the same and hard work will still be rewarded as always. There will still be fabulously wealthy individuals who own extravagant homes and luxuries that others cannot afford. Actually, as I have mentioned, getting to the point where you own four homes would be a goal to be accomplished because it comes with some pretty awesome benefits.

From an individual point of view, being different and going beyond means should matter most. By giving the necessities of their nations the ability to create money supply and also produce progressive technologies will bolster their economies and raise all standard of living around the world. Modern economic structures are holding us back from our true productive capacity by confining money supply to debt.

4.6.8.1 *Third World*

The mere fact that 'third world' countries is a term demonstrates the pure self-interest at hand in the global structure of bordered nations. Why is it that some countries are paid so much less than others? This classification could be described as supremacist. Labor is labor no matter which part of the world it's in. The fact that companies don't pay the same wages they would have to pay in their own country is immoral and unethical. Companies paint perfect pictures of themselves using corporate social responsibility reports, but when it comes down to it, if you're out there destroying the planet for a quick buck, there is no picture in which you are logically moral.

They see western nations as superior to others with no base other than they got lucky that many modern inventors have been American or European. So, no matter how they paint a rosy picture, the fact is corporations are harshly unethical by under paying third world locals because of a corrupt system of fixed exchange rates. They take advantage of a western supremacist worldview. Value statements and codes of practice come about because of the inherent unethical nature of business, which creates the need to manifest an image of being good when the reality is true morality is impossible to achieve with fractional reserve banking. If business were not inherently bad there would be no need for corporate social responsibility reports because nothing bad would ever happen. There is no need to prove you are good when you are indeed good.

4.6.9   Crime

In a world with a needs-based dollar crime would be greatly reduced. I find it highly probable that crime exists because of the truly difficult circumstances that this debt-based money supply system creates. It creates panic and stress in people by making the needs for survival scarce to the general public.

4.6.10   Luxuries Market

The luxuries market would consist of all other non-essential services and products. It would operate in the same fashion as it does today, except that the constant inflow of new money will come from the production of society's needs and the re-circulation of currency from firms that operate in the luxuries markets. This should create an atmosphere of abundance for humanity while creating an incentive to focus our primary efforts on the production of the necessities for the species. If the entire world could agree on this, we could really create an amazing vision of reality where suffering is a rarity. This system renders the federal government obsolete as it is seen today and so goes taxes in today's form as well. As previously mentioned, taxes on sales will be used as an anti-inflation measure during transition. These would be genuine free markets.

4.6.11 Basic Minimum Income

This idea, which has been floating around, is a patch-fix idea, that will ultimately fail to resolve the issues, because people will have the options of using that money for whatever they want instead of getting an appropriate credit of needs-based goods and services. It doesn't take into consideration the vast numbers of industries that are a need for the best survival of the species. Another problem is that in the current world where is that money going to come from? Will it be printed into creation? If so, inflation would be hard to control. My needs-based money supply system makes a lot more sense and is in the best interest of the species. Basic minimum income is an effortless idea that seems like the last dying breaths of an ancient inefficient system.

5 GOVERNMENT

Lincoln-"Government of the people, by the people, for the people, shall not perish from the earth."

5.1 PUBLIC AND PRIVATE LIFE

'Power tends to corrupt; absolute power corrupts absolutely. An observation that a person's sense of morality lessens as his or her power increases,' were words spoken by British Historian, Lord Acton, that leads me to question the divide in the public and private lives of politicians. Everyone is different in private than in public. There is no way to know what politicians think in private. What do you think of this divide between a politician's public and private behaviors? According to Lord Acton's logic, society should grant authority to more than one person.

We know that public image is manipulated and dressed to appear better than reality. When we look at our politicians, I find it best to use this kind of bs-cut-away-filter; "whatever they pose to be is a mere exaggeration if not complete dilution of their true reality; therefore, what they appear to be is far from what they are." If the public can see this fallacy in the political system, we can improve it. Why let the most manipulative people be in control of our laws and policies? Mass image manipulation is not the quality of a leader. Transparency is. One person becomes president with the help of many but takes credit for running a country that is mainly autonomous. Campaigning is a popularity contest for the rich who appeal to whatever fits their agenda.

5.1.1 Politician Liability

Politicians should be liable for bad actions or changes of promised actions once in office. This kind of liability needs to be in place for a system such as the one we have today. However, with a needs-based money supply system, the proper republic defining of government will be met. During the transition process into a needs-based dollar, government structures would stay in place, but as a malleable entity. This kind of change is slow and requires trial results.

5.2 MASS MEDIA ELECTIONS

Political broadcasting is a major business and is run by for-profit corporations that have strong bias favoritism when it comes to elections as anyone naturally would. Elections are conducted under the lens of the press leave voters at the whim of media conglomerates. Nations with modern population sizes should not use propaganda marketing campaigns. Simply put, mass media influenced voting creates a definition of government which is far from a republic one. Televisions and modern broadcasting was not around during the time of the declaration of independence which recognized natural law of humanities equality; therefore, could not have properly influenced the creation of modern systems which so heavily mimic the United States.

It is anti-democratic to use emotional appeal to gain votes. Votes are skewed by manipulative strategies seen in the media. A logical way of ridding the acquisition of votes based on perceived personal image bias is to never televise them. Having leaders be heavily publicized and glorified for the mere completion of their civic duties is highly anti-republican. For voters to control politicians, voters, should redefine what a politician is. Otherwise, voters should only be allowed to cast votes based on tests that prove they know what it is they are voting for, otherwise we risk having a leadership that consists of people who get there over the pure manipulation of their public image. In a needs-based dollar system, news broadcasting would be a needs-based service, which would protect it from bias and financial manipulation.

5.2.1   Modern Voting Process

For voters to cast their vote, they should have to have read the information folders and write simple tests that prove their knowledge of what they are voting for. Too often people vote based on candidates' personality or image regardless of what their political agendas are. That is what the constant two-sided election has done. This system has formed two sides for voters to align themselves with, regardless of future outcomes. Politicians get votes with unkept promises, because they know what voters want and they can trade votes for fake promises, for which they hold no liability. That's why politicians so often go back on their word, because they know that once they are in office, it becomes very difficult to reverse their actions. Not only that, the public hardly knows what it is they are even voting for.

These are pure manipulation tactics. It has allowed the most manipulative people in our societies to raise to the top of our power paradigm. We likely should ask ourselves if that is what we truly want in our leadership. How can we trust people that promise one thing and turn their backs? Can we not hold them responsible?

5.2.2   Influence of friends and family on votes

Because of friends and family, our votes may never be fully our own. We all grow up listening to our parents talk politics, and this has, in turn, an influence on our own views whether we like it or not. This is a bias influence that can lead us to want to join sides simply because our parents have done so, or we could also make the fallacy of taking a side only to oppose our parents. We can find ourselves aligning our beliefs in politics based on good and bad personal relationships, which is not appropriate rationale for such a decision.

5.2.3   Never Full Representation

Every election comes down to two people racing against each other... Does the country really split into those two ideologies? That cannot be true. If you are a believer in the modern voting system, think about this; have you in any of those times that you voted, fully agreed with everything the politician said? What many of you are likely to notice, is that there are in fact many things that we may not agree with. So, by choosing a side, are you really being represented or merely picking sides in a popular fad?

Voter participation numbers alone determine that proper representation at the level of specificity that governments have implemented, is not possible. Not everyone participates in the voting process. Right off the top we don't represent ineligible voters, which weeds out a bunch of people who may be tired of societal structures. Out of the eligible voters, often a little over half vote. Let's assume 60%. Because there is a portion of unrepresented people already by the 'ineligible voter' definition, we'll call it 50% of total possible voter's vote… okay, let's not give that consideration. Using 60% we still have 40% of eligible voters who did not vote, because they don't believe in what they see. An instant 40% of eligible voters are misrepresented off the top. After that about 31% of eligible voters elect the leader whose interest lay with his shareholders. Given this we see that about 69% of the population is being misrepresented. Chosen by the voters who are most easily influenced by public image manipulation. The real majority is the 40% who are sick and tired of the current structure. Forcing everyone to vote for things they don't fully understand won't work either.

5.2.4   Fundamental Laws

For representation to be met, society first should strip itself of self-interest-based rules and regulations so it is left with pure a form of moralism and ethics that all voters of a good nature would agree. People likely should stop trying to force others to bend to their belief's if they are not universally agreed upon.

1.   Treat others and their belongings the way you want

     others to treat you and your belongings.

     a.   No physical or severe mental abuse to others.

     b.   No theft.

     c.   No threat of harm.

2.   Government takes a passive republican definition of

     being a proponent of morality that is responsible for

the well-being of its citizens and guarantees their survivability without impeding individual sovereignty.

3. Law enforcement governing those three fundamental principles in section 1 would be essential services with funding protection.

5.2.5   Excessive Power

Too much power is given to the people who run nations. The last modification to the census was during the American Revolution when the founding fathers were worried of the corrupting nature of extended reigns over a nation. That is why George Washington did not want to be King. Instead, he created presidency. A revolutionary concept. Yet, here we are again with the need to redefine political leadership. It is time to demand the best for the species. With the needs-based money supply system this would happen as there would be less need for government officials in the sense that we have them today.

5.3 CORPORATE GOVERNMENT

Today governments are being run on a corporate model. I made this distinction in previous chapters; how the government sells the taxpayer or 'customer' services for monopolized pricing. Governments can now borrow money and pass the liability to taxpayers, which is the corporate veil that corporations' benefit from share ownership. Corporations are not Republics, they are for-profits, which is not a model you want for a Democratic Republic. So, government today is not the great populist entity that some imagine it to be. Rather, it is run like a high monopolized services corporation that has legal authority to price their services as proportions of your income at premium rates.

Knowing taxpayers will be liable for any future of the nation leaves immense room for moral hazard problems like politicians giving government contracts to friends or family at unfair rates. Why create this incentive for moral corruption if you don't have to? The problem with this image is clear, when governments start to use the population as a means to an end as do for-profit corporations, it fails to fulfill its responsibility as a republic democracy of making the population the end itself. Something that would be fixed by combining nations with the border agreements and a needs-based monetary system.

5.3.1   Taxation – Services Fees

Tax at its most fundamental level is unnecessary in a democratic republic. The only use for taxation is control in modern structures; therefore, a form of tax would still be used to decrease incentive to over accumulate real estate as mentioned before and anti-inflation measures. Why is it that money supply is created in the name of private banks instead of the common good? Well, banks will tell you that it allows for people to borrow and purchase the home of their dreams, but that benefit is really being generated by the banks. They spin it with the concept of the velocity of money and GDP-based nation states, but the truth is it is all based on psychologically damaging debt.

Think about it from the corporate government perspective. They put it on the people every year to count their transactions and organize everything themselves. The government makes it the people's duty to study countless complex unintuitive tax regulations to get any benefit. It became so complicated, that accountants are created around these areas of discipline in order to keep up with the number of rules. Studying accounting, for my undergraduate degree in finance and accounting, Tax was dense in material and content. Seems like all these rules were created in the spirit of more GDP through the creation of specialized jobs like accounts and tax specialists. Imagine getting rid of tax completely as we see it today, because we are an automated society… that is what the needs-based money supply system offers.

5.3.2   Tax as Counter-Productive.

Have you ever stopped to think about how many rules we are born into? On top of which, the rules are always expanding. They say, the only things that are certain are death and taxes, but we hardly need taxes for this new system of economy, because all the services governments provide us will be supported by money creation. Benefits we're giving to bankers will shift to the people.

Today, instead of spending time on taxes every year and record competing, people would have this time to focus on themselves providing a greater sense of liberty. I will also break down the divide between voters and the government. For the first time, our perspectives will be friendly. Taxes were reason for the revolutionary war in the States and will always be a proponent division between the people and government. If government is run like a corporation, then taxpayers are the customers, but the real people gaining the benefit are the shareholders behind the scenes. Any system that divides the population and contributes to the wealth distribution gaps is counterproductive to progress and unity. In this new system, because all the essential services and goods for society are taken care of through pure money creation based on a controllable inflation rate, we see that taxes would only be used as anti-inflation measures on sales taxes.

5.3.3   Tax as Form of Coercive Control

Today, tax is used to control populations, and greatly affects complacency in the masses. Tax authorities have the immoral right to imprint and steal from the population given they don't pay these monopolized fees. This kind of power is not only immoral; it is a fear tactic. By creating tax, you created entire immoral professions dedicated to enforcing them debt servitude. All to protect self-serving control and authority. Any institution that you owe obligation to and does not have your best interest in mind is by practical definition your master. This is counter intuitive because the masses are led to believe that they live in a democracy, but a true democracy would not create money and tax its people at the same time. Government exist to serve the people by being a component of logical morality instead of the people existing to serve the government.

5.3.4   Tax in a GDP Based Economy

Because governments rely on tax income, they create as much taxable production as possible in the economy regardless if they are efficient or not. To do this, they borrow money that is on the taxpayer. If you were insanely rich and held a bunch of government debt, and that debt was guaranteed by taxpayers who operate in an immoral debt servitude system, what would your incentive be? This will lead to the endless creation of counter-progressive jobs and tasks. For progress to be at its best we need to avoid redundant jobs processes and fines and prioritize a fully functioning automated society. Do you really want a government that is out to make as much tax revenue as possible and borrows from the world's wealthiest people on your behalf, but leaves you hanging when it comes to the bare necessities?

5.3.4.1 *Over-Bureaucracy*

The number of hoops people are required to jump becomes worse and worse in a GDP-debt model. Bureaucracy will always increase in complexity as time goes on. It is the nature of the GDP based economy coupled with the corporate structure of government that needs to change in order for bureaucracy to become efficient as well as effective.

5.4 CONCLUSIONS

Government should be a proponent of morality and welfare in society. At the moment the government does not see people as the ones they represent, instead they make people the labor force that creates GDP for their debtholders. This ropes back around to borders and competitive spirit of governments competing for the best production rate. Their focus will be on production not morality or the welfare of their citizens. In a world where automation is inevitable, we need to stop thinking at individual levels. We're all in this together.

5.4.1 Monarchies

In Canada, we have a constitutional monarchy and our money supply printing presses are called the royal Canadian mint. This ancient form of government is still accepted with complacency. A Royal family still holds rights to a Country where they do not live. This means that we, in Canada run a democracy in all its forms but the royal family must sign off on it. We are not one hundred percent sovereign. Everything is democratic except the final say. Given they are happy; they will sign off. I'm not saying that royalty did not play a vital role in our history and they deserve gratitude. However, for a civilization to truly utilize their resources and gain maximum benefit, we should cut them a break from their duties and allow them to be free wealthy individuals among the species. They should also understand that this is better for their own future generations survival as well. Does not mean they cannot enter the new forms of government if they so desire and achieve the positions. However, holding on to ancient traditions from times we know were so morally corrupt seems like we'd just be holding on to the past way of doing things, which creates such tension and divide among the species.

The royal family are far disconnected from the Canadian public as far as living perspective. Yet, they hold symbolic titles over the country and its people. Our officials are her employees running her responsibilities. Why is that we as a species cannot formally delete the symbolisms and ceremonial traditions of the past to move forward as we realize that the current paradigm is contrived, irrelevant, and outdated. The founding fathers introduced natural law to the world and got us all here, but they are not here to move us forward. We must do it ourselves. We must not hold onto old ideologies. Science can answer all superstitions.

In Canada final authority remains with the Crown and is entrusted to their government on behalf of the people, underlining the Crown's role in safeguarding the rights, freedoms, and democratic system of government of Canadians, and reinforcing the fact that "governments are the servants of the people and not the reverse." However, we have a government that is run under a corporate business structure in which the tax payer is the customer who ultimately pays the price in the form of promises of production while the publics needs for survival are left unmet. This quote 'that governments are the servants of the people' does not follow in a debt servitude system of money supply that turns tax payers into servants of the government. By the current model the tax payer serves the government and the government serves debtholders... interesting.

In a needs-based money supply system, royal families would maintain their objective wealth. They simply would not hold titles over sovereign nations by any means, iconic or otherwise. They would have all their assets converted and apply to all the same conversion rules as any other wealthy global citizen of the Global Union. Still means they maintain four to eight properties and have their money earn interest income enough for their future generations to never work. Especially when our priority is an automated world. My ideas are of non-violence and not pitchfork mob mentality ideas. I do not blame people born into vast wealth for something beyond their control, nor should we take away what is rightfully theirs in terms of wealth. However, hording of assets should be merely allowed in the form of currency or collectables but not real estate.

5.4.1.1 *Symbol, Titles, and Icons.*

Symbols have psychological effects on people's minds. We should not idolize other humans. We are all born the same by natural law. There should not be pictures of egos on coinage or currency. Everything should be unification orientated toward us being a multicultural species that considers morality in high regard. What is the point of this mass egocentric mindset of putting your brand on entire nations of people? The same traditions as our ancestors putting their emperors faces on the coinage of the time. These ancient ties to traditions and old ways of doing things holds us back mentally and morally. Symbols go back to the pyramids of Egypt. How we run every corporation and government. Pyramid systems. The fundamental structure for historical societies. We need to come up with something new a new order that symbols democracy at its richest and purest state and not authoritarianism. Because that is what we often see with royal Pictures and emblems. A depiction of triumphant euphoria. That is not to say things like the Pyramid should be destroyed… not at all. They are a symbol of progress.

5.4.2 New Landscape

What would a government look like in this new economic landscape? Since services they provide will be taken care of by necessities, federal officials will become groups of data analysts who have nothing to do with public relations. Elect leaders of the federal government the way we see it today would not be necessary. All territories in the global-union would share a basic set of laws based on the fundamental principle; treat others and their belongings the way you want others to treat you and your belongings.

- Don't Kill

- Don't Steal

- Don't Hurt People

*Any laws with other bases would be termed comprehensive laws and would be established by municipality.

5.4.2.1 *Democracy*

A system of government elected by the whole population or all the eligible members of a state, typically through elected representatives. Democracy is most representative concept for political operations to date, but we should always re-think how we operate our democracies when the populations have reached numbers never seen before.

5.4.2.2 *Federal Government*

The Columbia Encyclopedia defines government as "a system of social control under which the right to make laws, and the right to enforce them, is vested in a particular group in society". Not a single mention of morality... we likely should question whether our federal governments are appropriate the way we see them today. Current federal infrastructures would have to be used in the transition, as it's what we got. A federal government would only be established as a court system to rule on those laws governed by the golden principle. Those laws would only be reconsidered on evidence of moral error within it.

5.4.2.2.1 Military

The military would stay the same, however given how the system works, countries that agree to join the union would no longer need arms against each other. That does not mean the end of military research. Instead military research will be a necessity industry for society. An inter-union league of military games such as the Olympics would be established; national leagues should also be established. Annual games should be filmed and televised. That way we can keep the same defense infrastructures for military and training. The global union will use rubber bullets in the games an award the winners with cash prizes. Defense research spending should be balanced with terra forming and space exploration research. New weapon development should indeed continue as we never know what uncertain dangers may lay ahead. This could even be held as a decision making proves between countries who can basically bet on things over a non-violent skirmish. Really out there as these kinds of decisions should be left to the Main Council.

5.4.2.2.2 Federal Leadership

The whole concept of a single person running a large number of people is silly and not quantitatively representative. Federal leadership would be a council of non-elected individuals, but by academic, social, and moral merit. The council would consist of any odd number of individuals from the Global Union that can achieve this merit accomplishment and would be in charge of moral oversight. The number of members should be limited as should their term. Because they are of merit-based placement they have no legislative power to change law. More like think tanks for society, that would be paid a salary out of money creation. They would be assigned as independent advisors to elected municipal councils on a rotating pattern, being problem solvers for societal issues that develop, with the sole purpose of fostering morality and fairness. Federal officials would hold monthly conventions and self-organize these meetings. They would have the power to overturn any court ruling or comprehensive law within their regions, that they can prove to be immoral or abusive, given a majority vote is won. The federal leadership would have republic authority over any military action. Their authority would by that of states.

After federal leaders serve enough hours into the first level of federal leadership which would run five to ten years at the state or provincial level and proved their worth, they are promoted to Global Union Council. Main council is reserved for the entire union and works in a similar way as the provincial councils. The number should be odd and works in the same manner of member entrance; a different council member must be chosen. The main council will be limited and will only take in the most distinguished members as judged by their contributions and problems resolved during their terms. This leading council would act as overall advisors and councilors for society. They should be assigned to improving the society and diplomacy between the Global Union. Different councils for specializations would still be held. Their main objective would be to maintain peace within the union.

5.4.2.2.2.1 *Different Boards*

Different leadership boards would form based on group specializations. These boards would be assigned to their respective areas of the Global Union like boards of advisors.

5.4.2.2.2.2 *Merit Requirement*

These positions should hold heavy requirements of aptitude, critical thought, and academia. An example of something that I would use is four degrees in different academic fields. One must be in philosophy and another in political science. The other two degrees could be in anything. After those, a law degree must also be obtained. Oaths would be taken and a person would be entitled to a federal leadership position and salary. Because the number of federal officials must be odd, groups of two are required to enter, for which, declarations from both new members will be given vouching for the others honor; therefore, if one of them is later at fault of wrong doings, both may suffer consequence. This position would be on a one mistake you're out rule.

People who achieve this position would be very well compensated, but also held at a higher moral standard that others for this privilege. Graduates in engineering, sciences, or medicine would be assigned to the oversight of needs-based industries to reanalyze for efficiency and improvement. During the transition period, a group of established academic individuals would first be elected for these positions to be the initial federal leaders. After that it would become merit based. These would be the great minds of today. These leaders would also give periodic recorded lectures to the public and elected officials.

5.4.2.3 *Municipal Leadership*

Municipal leadership would not be structured with mayors at the top. Instead, one representative for every 100 people would be elected throughout cities by those 100 people. These would be chosen by vicinity. This elected person would get paid to meet all one hundred people they represent personally once a year to understand their needs. The next tier follows the same pattern. For every 100 1st tier representatives there will be a representative responsible for personally knowing those 100 1st tier representatives, which will also be elected by those 100 1st tier representatives. This would be repeated until a two-digit council is formed. For a city with population of thirty-three million, it follows; 33,000,000/100= 330,000 first tier representatives. 330,000/100= 3,300 second tier representatives. 3,300/100=33 third tier representatives. This would make representation a little more heard.

Each representative must hold at least one four-hour meeting a year with each person they represent. Their votes will count in the following sequence; the first and largest tier is closest to the people and will count as 4 votes each. The second tier would count as 7 votes each and the third tier would count as 13 votes each. Their duties are to vote on the comprehensive laws that are initiated into the decision-making process.

The initial group represented by first-tier representatives would not participate in those law passing votes. However, they would be the sole people responsible for initiating ideas to enter the decision-making voting process. The public would need a 65% favorable vote from the whole city population, excluding official representative votes, which would be done via mass messaging to the population to enter any new comprehensive legislation into the decision-making process.

Because of the ease of information, all ideas would have to be understood and confirmed by signature by every member of society via a confirmation application that reads it out to them. At first, every 100 eligible voters by vicinity would attend meetings to decide their representative and also whenever legislation is to pass that will affect them. This would only be required to pass comprehensive legislation not government by the federal courts governing the golden principle.

5.4.2.3.1 Merit for Municipal Leadership

These representatives will be compensated well but not as well as federal leadership as they will only require a single degree in any field to be eligible as a representative.

5.4.2.3.2 Meetings

Monthly meetings should be a requirement for every group of 100 eligible voters in which public affairs are addressed.

5.4.3 Justice System

Breaking the law is largely circumstantial. Few people fall into crime because they enjoy it. Most crime roots in the struggle for survival and in debt servitude. That is why a needs-based money supply system, abolishment of international borders, and legalization of recreational use of drugs for adults would obliterate crime. People would have their needs met. We should help those of unfortunate circumstances recover from the stresses that lead to crime. Likely, they have undergone much mental trauma. To kidnap them from their families and lock them in cages like animals is no different than how slaves were treated in the past. Especially when they are highly underpaid for heavy labor. I believe if every person is given the essentials of life; a permanent roof over their heads, the freedom of knowing their food and necessities are met, there would be few crimes. The only people that would commit crime in that environment are truly doing it out of bad intentions.

5.4.3.1.1 Motivations for crime

What is the average criminal's motivation? Normally it's financial, largely due to the combination of the needs luxuries markets. Furthermore, this single market is ruled by the debt-based dollar created by fractional reserve banking that breeds debt servitude. By taking away the motivational need for crime, there will be few crimes.

5.4.3.1.2 Drugs

Drugs also represent a large portion of crimes. Often behind drugs is money but not always. The most practical answer to the drug problem is obvious. Legalize and set up controls for the recreational use of them for adults above twenty-one. It is contradictory to allow opiates like oxytocin to be loosely prescribed and alcohol to be a legal drug monopoly.

The problem with the prohibition of drugs is that it will always create an illegal black market. Within this illegal black market there will always be inside players who take advantage of their positions to take part in the illegal money of trafficking drugs. This is contradictory because by fighting drugs we create a golem that gets bigger and stronger the longer we keep it illegal. The fact is that a demand exists to fuel black markets. Regulation only increases profit margins for criminals involved in the sale and distribution of narcotics around the world. I believe Amsterdam has the right idea in place for the control of narcotics. This would also add to the economy and allow new jobs and research to be conducted.

Legalization would create more businesses, more jobs, and alleviate stigmatic tensions drugs create between nations. People who are recreational use for adults will always be against those who are against it. It's a form of censorship. Wanting others to behave as you wish them to. That is not liberty. The reality is, as far as we know, that we only live once, and if adults want to experience drugs, that is their choice. Having a person completely disconnected from another come up with a rule based on their bias belief systems that allows for the imprisonment of that person based on possession over a substance is no different in mentality than a rapist who kidnaps his own daughter and locks them away. They both impede their own beliefs on others.

5.4.3.1.3 Opioid epidemic

Across the United States and Canada, we see increasing deaths and addiction cases due to OxyContin and fentanyl. People are dying left and right. I constantly read how ambulances are kept so busy with the down town east side drug users overdosing and relying on their services to shoot them with the anecdote. Users knowingly overdose... this problem is not due to illegal street drugs made in underground labs, it is mass producing pharmaceutical companies and doctors over prescribing these drugs for money. But we don't see anything being done about those drug dealers. I blame this immoral behavior on the deterministic aspects that a debt-based dollar fractional reserve system creates in society. The struggle is too much for some and they chase the quick high that drugs provide so they can stop thinking about how awful the world is. Yet, pharmaceutical companies and doctors themselves are responsible for the deaths of millions of people due to their over prescription. Instead, they profiteer off it. These markets would be considered fully luxury and not benefited from the needs-based money supply system.

5.4.3.1.4 Gun Control

Once they are around, they are difficult to take away. Guns disappear into the underworld every day. This is largely done for financial gain. With people's needs being taken care this sort of behavior would be a lot less incentivized. There should be no issue with owning guns for marksmanship and hunting use if we live in a highly moral society that doesn't exclude anyone from the necessities of life; given they are mentally stable. The need to have guns for security purposes would likely go down in such a system as well.

5.4.3.1.5 Prison System

The prison systems operate as a close form of modern slavery. People are made to work laborious jobs which they are paid very little for. Then when they are back in society they are forced into those same laborious jobs. In many instances for drug charges without a violent nature. Yet, they are forced into the same brutal inhuman punishment that makes the punishers much worse than those being punished by moral standards. Especially when a crime is committed on the basis of survival, which should be taken care of in the first place.

The concept imprisonment as a form of punishment is ancient and outdated. How are prisons different than a person who kidnaps an innocent person to hold captive in small quarters? Logically we are not other than the fact that we imposed our views of punishment on them which are immoral to say the least. People who break the golden principle laws that cover murder, rape, and battery are likely the people who need help the most. Imprisoning them in immoral conditions is not teaching them anything but hatred. However, I do believe that such heinous criminals should be isolated from the general public for treatment. Theft is a crime that should be separate from those three of murder, rape, and battery; therefore; should be treated differently. Facilities for all violent criminals are well established in Norway where inmates live together. Inmates should be educated in Moral Philosophy and Law. Any criminal guilty of murder, rape, or battery specifically should require a microchip implant to track them upon release.

They should be aware that the chip tracks their every move. A small sacrifice for freedom if one has committed such a crime; a sacrifice which would have to be earned through reasonable proof of change.

5.4.3.1.6 Unleveled Consequences

Theft or drug possession does not equal the psychological damage of being branded as cattle. This view of the human being as beast of burden is primitive and dated for such a modern civilization. Old legal precedents that have become irrelevant should nullify as times change. The justice system displays some philosophical issues in how we operate that remind me of the Salem witch trial mentality. For example, how society perceives a person who kidnaps a woman and locks her in a dungeon within his basement. Let's say the person has a steady job and no one ever finds out. In Austria some crazy 73-year-old man kept his daughter locked up so he could rape her. If he didn't rape her but merely locked her up that would still be perceived as evil and torturous. On top of which some inmates are raped in prison and suffer very similar psychological trauma as that man's daughter. There is not much difference from that to locking people in a medieval style penitentiary for committing petty survival-based crimes. Neither of which reach the heinous nature of forced captivity. The justice system inflicts forced captivity on countless people for crimes that are not nearly deserving of such consequences. How can someone even compare being locked away and possessing a substance subjectively considered illegal by governments that elected by 31ish percent of eligible voters?

5.4.3.1.7 Breed Hate and Divide of Incarceration

Tension and divide is a consistent theme of current societal structures. When put someone through medieval captivity and break them down; you are being no different morally than those criminals themselves, which creates tension and divide between the victims of human punishment and the punishers. This sort of captivity should not be used on anyone that is not irrationally violent as logic dictates you are worse than your victims. Psychological damage, the system takes people and does serious mental damage. They mold people into hardened or broken people with major trust and authority issues.

5.4.3.1.8 Detention

5.4.3.1.8.1   Violent offenders

Have any offender of a violent crime, such as murder and rape be inserted with a tracking device after rehabilitation. They must not know the position of these devices within their bodies. Criminals that never qualify as rehabilitated should be transferred to enclosed farms or neighborhoods with nature and amenities where the inmates rule themselves but cannot leave a large premise. Also, should be tracked with an implant. Commodity production would be encouraged. They could even run their own small enclosed ethical farms if desired and proof trustworthy. Otherwise a prison system with less medieval quarters should be used. We see this in some countries throughout Europe, which is a great step in an ethically moral direction.

5.4.3.1.8.2   Theft

Theft should be punished in the person making mandatory repayments of double value back to the person. If amounts are very high a permanent lifetime future earnings deduction could be implemented. However, the replacement of fractional reserve banking with a needs-based money supply model would likely eliminate most need for theft to occur as it is my hypothesis that people mainly steal over the struggle for survival created by the debt-based dollar.

5.4.3.1.9 Law Enforcement

Police enforcement and military is something long embedded in society. These are not only hugely apart of our societal structures, but they are essential to our safety and future survival. Regulation of the basic fundamental rules should be enforced by a police force that is not always out in public in uniform. Instead, a designated number per 100 represented people would attend community meetings in regular clothing. Because these laws will mainly focus on theft and violent crimes, these officers would hold concealed weapon permits and drive unmarked cars. These would also be the officers responsible for house calls.

5.4.3.1.9.1 *Bylaw officials*

These kinds of officers would resemble modern police but they do not carry guns on their body, just pepper spray, baton, and Taser. Guns would be prohibited to the trunks of their marked cars. They would have authority over bylaws and traffic laws only. They would however not serve a function in larger investigative functions, which would be reserved to the casual clothes investigators which must earn a degree in criminology and psychology. Bylaw officials must however still have to undergo training.

5.4.3.1.9.2 *Authority*

Law Enforcement would answer to federal leader boards and court judges. The court systems of today would stay highly the same as would the military, other than war within the Global Union constrained to the War Games which do not use live ammunition. The Military would also be in charge of any large violent civil unrest within the Global Union. Though it is likely to never occur given full realization of such a plan. The purpose of this model is to preserve whatever structures we can, by simply making small adjustments for efficiency.

6 EDUCATION

Confucius – "I hear and I forget. I see and I remember. I do and I Understand."

6.1 CHANGING ENVIRONMENT

As with the rest of this book's theme, education has to deal with the internet's effect on public access to information as much as any societal structure. Furthermore, it is the educational system that requires most adaption to such an advent and should be perceived and welcomed as beneficial. This may be redundant to all of you, but back in the day, when there was no internet, it was a difficult task to find information. Today, we simply access our collective information with smart phones in our pockets. So how relevant is most of the material at school when we can walk into a job with a smart phone, and likely pick up most of the immediate practical skills and know-how on the go?

The past structures were set up with this adverse access to information in mind, which assumes people are heavily reliant on expert opinions and authorities. This has contributed to a society being created with heavy reliance on the authority fallacy. Today, jargon, or specialized words in specific industries, is scattered through Film and Television. A fictional experience that applies to life can teach as well as a real-life experience in my opinion. However, individuals perceive things differently; thus, learn different lessons from the same story.

Because access to information was a barrier to entry for knowledge of professions. Today, these barriers still exist, and this profit-oriented business structure for education systems, is a hindrance to genuine education. So-called 'public school' systems operate on the premise of charging tuitions in the forms of interest bearing student loans or cash an attempt to make a profit. Don't let government subsidies misguide you into thinking public universities aren't for-profit businesses using students as a means to an end. Remind you of anything else?

6.2 EDUCATION ORIGINS

Forms of schools existed as far back as 1500 BCE with the Indian Vedic period. Teachings were places that taught moralism and spirituality, which correlates back to the topic of religion and its origins. Back then it was reserved for people of privilege and high social classes. China had five national schools during the Zhou dynasty from 1045 BCE to 256 BCE. There, the educational system was developed to help build the empire by teaching morality among others. In Greece people had to pay for education. What we see is that all societies find education beneficial for progress, which should be intuitive. Around the 16th century, we began to educate more like we do today.

6.3 CRITICAL THOUGHT AND MEMORY

Modern school curriculums are so heavily short-term memorization based, that we may be missing out on the opportunity to enhance natural brain evolution through education. Don't get me wrong… there is great benefit in having a large knowledge base of practical facts to draw upon in everyday life and business. My argument is that section should be completely left toward to later time in a person's life, after having developed their brains to their maximum capacity. First, we should develop their brains within an environment of enhanced critical though. Especially during those ever so important early years. We have a blessing with this portion of our children's molding and indeed, we have so much time in which to influence children's minds until adulthood that we could develop each human under circumstances for them to be equipped with the most evolved mind that one could have. If we want to exceed the limits that we give ourselves, we likely should develop children's brains for maximum capacity first. What does that mean? Critical thought puzzles, memory improving techniques, efficient learning, natural law, and understanding logic and reason. Subjects rarely if ever seen in early elementary school.

6.4 SCHOOL SYSTEM

Today, school systems are mental conditioning facilities. If we're going to do this, we might as well use it to proactively enhance brain evolution. School systems in general teach a rigid framework that holds consequences. It is fear-based education instead of curiosity driven from the start. We designed schools to be this way for kids to condition them for a future working life. What they should do is teach our children to use their brains efficiently with techniques to maximize potential all the way up to at least grade eight.

6.4.1   Authoritarianism

We are conditioned to be complacent to an authority figure instead of developing our own ideas in independent thought. True, it is nearly impossible to avoid an authority figure given we all have parents who embrace an authoritarian image. However difficult this approach is to break, it runs the risk of driving our children from us. We should see them as our reincarnations, and only then can we start treat them as equals from the start, but the authoritarianism has deep roots in ancient social structures. Change starts with teaching children reason and logic early in life and encourage independent thought. There is anything that we can all agree on is reason and logic should guide our decision-making process. Logic is universal and can convince anyone who understands it; therefore, logic should be our authority.

Ingrained authoritarian structures makes it easy for power and money to consolidate into a fewer hands. The authoritarian mindset education conditions into our minds to be complacent. Authoritarianism breeds complacency, which is a kryptonite to innovation. Yet, nothing has gotten us further than innovation and anti-authoritarianism. Throughout history, brains and psychology have evolved accustomed to this authoritarian environment and undoing the damage will not be easy. The process takes generations and its initiators would never see their results. Today, we are so used to authority that it has infested every aspect of life. Even when we google answers to things, we are looking to an informative authority.

Students look to experts for solutions instead of thinking of them critically. From an early age, we go to school, which imprints the idea that an authority knows that answer. It may not be until we are much older that we notice the flaws in other adults, but as children with a blank slate, we are being bred into a system that always has an authority. It is no coincidence that government operates in the same pinnacle structure that looks up to an authority. Corporations with CEO's. When you break it down further, it always centers on a prime alpha position instead of council. In a needs-based money supply system this will change as education becomes an essentials industry.

6.5 CONCLUSIONS

Liberty is not considered for children in current culture. Adults are the ones for which liberty applies nowadays. Do you agree? So, if we're going to do this, we might as well implement the most beneficial brain development structures for our children. I'm profoundly fond of education, but fear it misses out on proactively participating in enhancing natural evolution. At a young age we are trained to comply with authoritarian structures that resemble later political and business power paradigms. Can this be a coincidence? Likely not. It's how we evolved, thus, changing requires radical outside-the-box thought on everyone's behave, and the result is worthwhile; the betterment of our species. With education entered into the needs category of a society run by my needs-based-money supply system, education would seize to operate in a profit-oriented corporate structure that uses students as a means and fulfill its noble purpose of developing minds to their greatest potential. Human beings should have the time and liberty to develop their minds, because in needs-based-money-supply system automation would be categorized as a human need eventually rendering menial labor completely obsolete.

Funny how group work in school will be pushed on curriculums especially in business, which is my concentration. Seems like professors just don't want to do as much work so they condense the amount of work that has to be graded in the form of group projects. Complacency within the education system is alive and well. Education for profit is not a good system for teaching and advancing our species.

A fundamental need of education, lies in critical thought and logic-based thinking. If a person can be taught to think critically and abstractly to solve issues with a well-trained logic in the mind there is no task, industry, or job that they cannot easily get proficient at within a period of one year. They should have proven to think critically and understand the concepts of logic. Teaching children to teach themselves efficiently and problem solve with logic and reason is what school systems need deeply ingrained in our children early for beneficial evolution. Imagine what our minds would be like in a thousand years if we evolved with these teachings early.

6.5.1   Evolution

I'm no evolutionary expert but it seems that we should consider the portion of our lives from birth to having children to be crucially important steps in the process of natural evolution. Because every experience, event, and exercise we do before we have children will influence the genetic code we pass down. Logic seems to follow that the longer we live a healthy proactive life before having kids, the better results we'll see from evolution. The more experience we pass down, the better the genetic code. In a society where inactivity is so easily achieved, there lies greater responsibility on us to proactively enhance evolution. We should not only exercise regularly, but persistently develop our brain capacities. Any progress we make for our genetics after we have kids is merely irrelevant to natural evolution.

6.5.2   Early Education

Birth through to the end of high school is a critical portion of a child's developmental process. Truth is, when we review educational history, we notice education has led progress in all aspects whether it be institution or self-pursued. If we want material proof of this benefit, we have to look no further than the technologies we hold today; given to us by the great academic minds of our past. We have to look no further than Isaac newton, Socrates, or Marie Curie.

Imagine we had the most efficient forms of education. Surely, we currently hold ourselves back. The comparison I would makes is with runners. Athletes who run 100 miles, whom before had never attempted that distance, prove incredible lessons in self-limitations. Our minds self-limit potential if we are complacent. Today, we have grown in an environment that contrives us to underestimate our own potential, not only physically but intellectually. If we desire optimal results from our actions, we should apply this concept to every aspect of life. Especially, in forming our children's minds. We certainly have the potential to achieve beyond what the current systems require of us at early ages. Of course, that is not to say that people would not be free to pursue any educational structure they implement for their children in a free society.

Brain development during learned communication stages and early school are crucial points in children's lives that significantly influences their future intellectual capacity for memory, critical thought, and creativity. This period can make a 'genius,' or maximum capacity brain if subjected to the right external stimuli and situations. We should first develop children's brains to enjoy curiosity and teach them mental tools of efficient learning and memory retrieval. Current educational structures focus on determined facts and history too early on in a child's development. Things like memory development techniques, efficient learning techniques, and critical thought puzzles, should be introduced firsts.

Through the practice of this, they will be taught discipline. Children should be guided to develop inclinations to independence, self-sustainability, and self-growth. Instead of asking for answers they should be taught to solve problems. In a system where they first learn to maximize their brain capacities, that systems worst academic performer would likely outperform many of the best in the current system. It should start early during brain development to activate our potential.

6.5.2.1 *Teachings*

A child's first learnt concept would most beneficially be visualization techniques. Upon waking and before bed will ingrain discipline and enhance cognitive and memory capacities. Since the first years of a new born is a stage when parents educate kids without external institutions, parents have the responsibility to reinforce these invaluable practices. Since, Darwin introduced evolution, it is our responsibility to discover our influence in natural evolution during one life-time. That is, if we want the best results.

The best enhancement for a child is natural. It lies in regular exercise of mind and body. I find it probable, that giving children active meditative-visualizations as a first concept, will link abstract connections in their brains that develop early multi-leveled thought, that will ingrain in evolution. Getting a child to practice and understand meditative visualization early is the best thing for their memory capacity and a more active brain in general. Strong belief systems will mold a strong mind, and likely have beneficial evolutionary effects on the human brain if persistently practiced for many generations. When we are infants, parents can manipulate all of the events in our lives, which are the events that will inherently mold belief systems. Instill early on, powerful life teachings that would normally be reserved for us at later ages. Especially in critical thought and moral philosophy. We think leaving them naive in fantasy world is healthy, but the reality is, we're on a long-term time clock waiting for the inevitable moment of extinction unless we do something about it. Creativity will be more greatly developed with meditative-visualizations. Life is not a fantasy wonderland, but a tough complex landscape. Our children should not have things kept from them. If their brains process things earlier, they will reach a stage of self-awareness and enlightenment faster than anyone today, while their brains develop to greater capacities.

What kids need to learn early on, is control of their minds through strong critical thought exercise and visualization. Guiding kids to exercise these practices early and daily will strengthen self-discipline. Teach kids early that achieving a near perfect memory, if not a perfect one, is something learnt, so that it becomes a common occurrence. If we institute these positive habits early in our children's lives, they would likely grow more competent than we could ever reach in the rest of our life spans. Being that children have a malleable mind for belief systems is a once-in-a-life-time occurrence for us to mold their minds to max capacity. Like science talks about how giving your infant, touch, affects them later in life, these exercises and activities will greatly affect their competence and brain capacity. Creativity and memory will be nothing like anything we have ever seen; especially, after multiple generations.

Think of children as reincarnations of yourself, would you not want to develop your own mind for maximum potential if you had a chance to mold your development early on? Well that is quite literally what this is. Science should prove that newborns are DNA re-creations of their parents. The question is not whether we are physical reincarnations, but whether our current conscious reincarnates when we die as well.

Daily visual development practice can be done with two thirty minute sessions a day. More would be better if the child finds pleasure it doing so. We don't want to over burden a child to resent the practice. Positive reinforcement should be attached to the experience to make it desirable. It is crucial to make the exercise fun by linking it with a positive reward system that creates nostalgia, so in the future the discipline associates well with them. I would set the same times every day; upon waking up and before bed. Sit and focus on breathing while having eyes closed. Enter a slight hypnotic trance by visualize and verbally counting down from ten or twenty, then suggest they visualize anything they desire. Suggest landscapes or images of known interest to the child. Inform them they can control this landscape in their minds. Eventually teach them that the functions of their minds including habits can be formed and re-molded by coming to their special mental place created by visualization.

During the first 365 sessions twice a day, the child should have developed significant visual landscapes. This first year, every visualization should be creative and freely developed allowing the child to roam in the visual landscape that you create with them as they see fit. During year two, you want to add structures such as building or permanent abode in the child's mind. You will in intervals add different rooms, floors, furniture, and objects with assigned functions within this dwelling. If you feel the child is ready to start this sooner and shows interest in doing so, you should encourage this. Examples of the different room or object functions should have links to relaxation, regeneration, memory storage, memory recollection, and mood control. Examples of these could be rooms, pools, theatre, whatever you find useful to the functions. Most importantly, the visualization room. Imagine this room like a theatre where the child sits as the audience and creates objects on the stage. The memory room is also important because it is where the children can store specific memories that are important to them. Most who apply this technique like to use a library with books that contain all different associative images. It could also be a DVD collection room in which each DVD represents a running memory. This is a crucially important room that will build the ease of memory recollection. A mood room can be used to control anxieties and anger when they are stimulated by the environment. The conscious and subconscious mind will automatically do these things in real-time in milliseconds after years of this meditative practice.

In the third year, visualization puzzles should be introduced into the daily exercise. This will lead to cognitive benefits. Still avoid teaching them too many facts that are not relative to their natural living environments. Facts and history is plentiful and highly developed superior minds will learn them at accelerated rates later in life. Learning how to use their minds to improve themselves and become self-aware early is the most beneficial start. If visualization techniques can become enhanced and continued through school systems, that would be the most beneficial. This sort of daily visualization exercise should be done all the way until the brain has fully developed into adulthood, at which point the daily exercise can be relaxed and used only when desired. However, persistent use of it until you choose to parent another child will lead the greatest evolutionary benefit for the new genome.

6.5.2.1.1 A Child's First Concept Reiterated

Today, there is a garden variety of different memory techniques that you can explore with a google search, but here is what I believe is the most beneficial. Sit down with a child as early as possible in their life, that they can comprehend this and focus on breathing for five minutes by narrating a relaxation method for breath, such as light entering and leaving their body with every breath. Follow by adding a vivid picturesque scene and asking them to add things. This should start as soon as the child is able to grasp the concept. Not only are they benefiting, but you are benefiting. It is never too late to work on aspects of ourselves. Evolution does not take a break. Their first sentences and understandings should be deep fundamental concepts of life. They should understand the mechanics of their minds early, so they are taught to be self-aware before they get to school where they interact with others.

Habits are difficult to develop and get rid of; therefore, meditative-visualization should be the first concept our children learn. This practice will teach them self-control as a fundamental concept while improving creativity and memory capacities. You want to give a child liberty with their time around these activities, but they need a positive structure of self-improvement as a first concept. This will ultimately flip Maslow's hierarchy of needs upside down.

After three or four years of this 30-minute twice a day exercise, the child will have a strong visual mind. By this time, the child should be nearing the age of five, six, or seven for which reading should be greatly simplified. It would be interesting to see all the creative scenes they imagine or 'remembered,' that we likely should document. This would investigate any possibility of passed memories that may be stored in DNA, regardless any improbability attached. If investigating it will benefit that child's intellectual evolution, why not do it? I find it highly probable that we can access information our conscious is not immediately aware, which is where new ideas come from.

6.5.3   Institutional Education

*Subjects should be taught in-depth by focusing on one subject at a time for extended terms.

6.5.3.1 *Elementary School Grades 1 - 4*

This period is crucial for children to continue their visualization training. At this point, children should begin learning formal higher-level memorization techniques, critical thought puzzles, efficient learning skills, evolution, writing, reading, philosophy, moralism, racism, psychology, and discrimination. All of these should be reinforced and practiced in-depth within these four years. Positive reward systems should be implemented.

6.5.3.2 *Elementary School Grades 5-8*

During this period, children should continue daily meditative visualizations with enhanced memory techniques. Education should focus studies on health nutrition, math, astronomy, biology, physics, engineering, and environment.

6.5.3.3 *High School Grade 9-12*

This is the time to teach them societal structures, history, politics, laws, business, economics, and other practical life skills. Meditative visualizations should continue daily. Children that have gone through this sort of education system will be well equipped for entry level positions in many fields by the time they are finished high school.

6.5.3.4 *Post-Secondary*

At this point students could would likely go through University degrees at accelerated rates with ease. If citizens desire to work and leave the pursuit of knowledge, they would be learnt enough to enter many entry level positions. Post-secondary would be for people who want to research further and also is a requirement for many new positions that accompany a needs-based money supply model. As outlined above federal leadership positions would require four degrees. These requirements are malleable and should be further considered if such a model is implemented. The goal of this educational model is to equip ourselves to max potential and proactively enhance natural evolution.

6.5.4 **Student Loans**

Loans are clear instruments of a debt-based monetary system. This is a scheme set up by debt holders. Student loans become in the profit view of government a form of making money on education. The psychological pressure of debt is enough to crush people working while studding is efficient for the efficient learning. If students are not lucky enough to have their parents pay their academic lifestyles, they have to indebt themselves or work to save up for school. The structure of society is to have students pay for educations that are meant to serve the government's goal of GDP creation because it increases the labor force, which in turn generates revenue for their monopolized services model. Proof of how the government uses citizens as means to an end. Who really gains the benefit? The governments debtholders; or the world's wealthiest, the only people who can live off of the rates governments offer. Students are being used as a means to the end for a corporate government structure rather than being the end.

This is the consequence of running a competitive GDP based economy on fractional reserve banking, because the main focus of education becomes to generate GDP or profit for the government who owes the wealthiest people a ton of money. The only reason they are rich is because we, the people made them so. We buy degrees and only a small portion of us use that them. Do we get a refund? Not from the government. The only benefactor is the government no matter how it turns out for you. Whether the degree lands you a job or not the government gets its cut and the debtholders get their interest. If you work menial jobs to pay for it, governments get their GDP and their tax income, while you are left to struggle for your own best survival; something the government is elected to provide.

We have an economic and political combination that forces us to work off interest bearing debts in order to expand our own money supply, then it wants us to accelerate the velocity of money like rats on a wheel. A smoke screen is created by allowing anyone to purchasing government debt; which creates a second-tier class structure. The mental suffering that debt has is a burden on the mind that feels like a ton of bricks on your shoulders. In the United States subconscious manipulation of placing a public debt counter for everyone to see sends the subliminal message that every family is in debt. Student loans are simply another form of condition to the human mind, to be complacent to debt structures.

6.5.5　Separation

Education was a system of separation of classes in the past as much as it is in the present. Today different schools exist for different classes of wealth. We are not working together to learn and nourish collective knowledge for the benefit of the species. It seems to nourish separation and secrecy; therefore, is self-serving. Today, education is a way people get ahead, because it gets them paid. It has continued to serve societal status. Education should unite us and be an all-around beneficial experience for everyone. This separation fosters using education as a means to an end instead of education being the end itself.

6.5.5.1　Money Driven Education and Status

Profit　models　for　educational　institutions　incentivizes

professors to skew results regardless of ability to protect their image and income. Given tuitions are paid and classes attended with minimum effort, students get a degree. Students don't generally want to study. Often, they are pushed into a career by the parents who were influence by societal structures. They want to pass school without much effort and when they get A's, too often, hubris egos are created. Because kids want to slack and pass classes easily, professors have pressure to easy up on students and skew grades. Going through university often, professors eliminate questions students had problems with on exams to improve overall grades, because if students turn in low grades people may downgrade the school meaning less tuitions.

This profit model is anti-educational and hinders the species. Often, I found group situations in which those who earn grades are forced to share results with students who did not contribute. Therefore; many university graduates have little credibility. My university attendance showed me that giving 40-75% effort at school would likely get me a 70%-75% grade. No matter how much effort I put into some classes, some professors would give me the exact same grade across the board. Not all professors are like this. Some were great and you could tell which ones really enjoyed academia.

6.5.6   The Great Library Concept

Likely not the great library you are thinking of, but rather, a concept for higher learning around the world. I pose that all University rooms be equipped with video and audio recording, then connected to a live global stream that is open to the Global Union ruled by a needs-based money supply system. Imagine at all moments of the day, live lectures stream somewhere in different languages. A Great Library Concept would maximize potential in humanity and accelerate progress. People may learn multiple languages with live lectures happening worldwide every minute of the day. This would integrate cultural diversity and compliment an open border world; therefore, the network should only be accessible to nations that have open border agreements with each other. A centralized database would accurately document educational life; the kind of big data that we need to be collecting.

This would be more easily instituted in multinational conglomerates like the EU. Since they have gone as far as to unify their currency, they could easily form this concept. Countries that resist the idea of merging their borders and separating their needs and luxuries markets would be excluded from the use of these systems. It may seem contradictory to divide the Global Union from debt-based money supply system run nations, but that is for the sole purpose of uniting the world. As the Global Union gets bigger anyone left out would have it at their best interest to join the needs-based monetary supply system.

6.5.6.1 *Agreement for Cultural Convergence.*

This concept would lead to eventual cultural convergence which means populations would easily learn the different cultural within the Global Union by simply watching lectures. Learning new languages would be made hugely more efficient.

6.5.6.2 *Open Tests*

Open test sessions for self-taught students would be made available in all nations under this agreement. These tests would be held on a weekly or quarterly basis depending on demand of such tests that would be tracked with statistical data from pre-registers and attendees. This would allow for any self-motivated student within such a multinational conglomerate to earn degrees if disciplined enough to do so on their time and cost free.

For this system to work we would require lecture presenters and classes participants all funded by the needs-based money supply system. I would go as far as to make interactive learning sessions for each class and have students earning their degrees to participate in videos. Activities like debates and intellectual competitions. We should push our minds regardless of how uncomfortable. If a puzzle seems complicated it is because you are out of practice or simply because the creators mind and yours are not alike. When you begin to understand their methods of developing things like Mensa puzzles, then the puzzles become easy themselves.

6.5.7 Importance and Value to Society

The education institution should be the most revered institution of humanity. Any laborious work should will replaced with automation, so humans are left to a lifetime of the pursuit of knowledge or simply to enjoy the miracle that is life. From my experience at university, I felt not only gender bias but discrimination occur. I find it surprising that at the advent of film recording, the first idea was not to record every lecture ever given and compiling a library. Some companies have taken to doing this, such as the teach yourself company, but again, that was profit orientated.

6.5.8   Necessity of life

Education is backbone of the progress and likely should be held in high regard. Education and higher learning would be the central focus of human beings in an autonomous labor society. We would not want AI that could over power us; instead, humanity would be the seed of ingenuity. For a perfect society of this nature, automation would convert to needs-based along with education. Lecturer titles would be earned and lectures paid for each lecture given by the needs-based money supply system. Rates would be variable according to stable inflation. Without trial results exact inflation stability controls cannot relevantly be construed.

7 SCIENCE AND TECHNOLOGY

A.P.J Abdul Kalam "Science is beautiful gift to humanity: we should not distort it."

7.1 CLASSIFICATIONS

Innovation within science has been the leading aspects of progress. For the most part, major technological changes are usually thought of in terms of mechanics or online based. However, things like religion, tradition, and education, can be described as social technologies. We are so fascinated by engineering's mechanical gadgets, that we neglect to focus on social technologies and paradigms that are established, when in fact these social technologies are likely to provide beneficial improvements in every aspect of our society including science and technology.

Late developments in these social technologies have nobly fought inequality. There is still abundant excess of inequality scattered across earth, and next in line is the elimination of human-based physical labor. Realization that we are made of the same biological matter, has shown itself in recent history. Yet, leaders like Martin Luther King have been assassinated for promoting human equality, which proves the existence of human forces that want to hold the current paradigm in place. Surely that is not questioned in any rational adult's mind at this point in time.

All our progress has been thanks to scientists and philosophers of the past, not often wealth holders and policy makers. Understanding the universe and its laws have shown themselves to select minds who have bestowed the knowledge and responsibilities of it on society and led to all the marvels we have today. In the beginning, survival drove technology. The wheel, fire, writing, spoken language, all survival-based technologies; which with time changed from being survival-based to becoming greed-based. What we see are creations by for-profit organizations who merely care about self-gain. A lot of inventions that serve no need of the human, but rather the luxury desires of consumers. There is nothing wrong with it given we have our priorities in order. Fact is, resource on earth is scarce, and for a race with a definite end, we should heavily consider the priority of our resource allocation. As of now the species is failing to prioritize what is most crucial to its survival. There is no blame: rather, opportunity exists to learn.

Logic follows, at least from my perspective, that survival-based technology should be prioritized. At least until we can secure additional resource outside of earth. From my perspective, technology should also split into needs and luxury classifications as with every other product or service in my needs-based-monetary system. Technologies that serve society's survival should be classified under necessities and be allowed the benefit of having money be created by its viable demand. Examples of these would be all automation, weapons, robotics, space exploration, mining, and agricultural equipment. This would be a gradual build contingent upon anti-inflation measures as mentioned before.

This classification would not only create incentives for people to invent things but would make it so that any product that ever came into existence aiding the species would never be suppressed. Instead, nations within the global union would work on these industries as a team. Of course, the exact mechanics, regulators, agencies, regulations, and policies regarding such a system would require dramatic restructuring and reform that would likely take multiple generations to materialize. Especially in a heavily bureaucratic system that has rooted itself in our society.

7.2 PERCEPTIONS

Having society witness advents of airplanes, motor-cars, and lifts, as spectacles, changed the way masses perceive possibilities. In the past, machines aided human self-reflection. Modern literature and art, technology does the opposite; being so embedded in our culture, technology lost its glowing essence of novelty since the early century. We can hardly imagine what it's like to live in a world without conventional technology. It's astounding how little of the natural world is a part of our lives in first world nations. Especially, with the internet spreading into every corner of the globe.

Today, people who are glued to their cell phones have less and less time to reflect on themselves. A fear of being alone and in isolation with our thoughts exists within new generations; one that could have severe consequences on brain evolution. Much has changed since telephones allowed us to self-reflect, and now, when a cell phone runs large portions of people's thought-process through visual gratifications. However, it not only serves as a proficient tool, it can encourage self-reflective thought for those of us who can step away from the addicting allure that it provides.

How much of our psychology is defined by our technology? Millenniums of global tensions that led to the cold war and subsequent resource wars for oil from the Persian Gulf to Iraq has desensitized the general population to violence. Desensitization has significant influences on the human psychology. Symptoms of this show up in the forms of school shootings, wrongdoing cults, and serial killers. Violence has a profound presence on what we watch for entertainment; and shows up everywhere from video games to film and television.

From when we wake up in our tantra-pedic mattresses to drive our electric cars to our destinations or when we brush our teeth, technology has molded every aspect of our daily habits. exercising requires the quality of shoes and clothing. Running barefoot on bare ground is hardly considerable anymore. Having life set to be so predictable is something that technology has encouraged. Without its progressions life was laborious. Hunting, gathering, or farming was necessary; however, those were novel technologies in their advent, difference being they required physical exercise and took extended portions of our days. Journeys of hunting and gathering took all the sunlight.

Today it takes 30 minutes to stock a fridge up with a few weeks supply of food. A feat unimaginable two hundred years ago. The home refrigerator was invented in 1913 and likely one of the most ground-breaking technologies to that changed the way in which we viewed survival. From a long tedious workday to setting décor for a dinner party, technology has massively changed our daily habits. However, it has been since the internet and cell phones that dramatic differences appeared. Arguments for both good and bad exist since modern technology is so groundbreaking and cutting edge. The truth is, we are test subjects. Will our habits change? Our sexual desires? With internet and pornography so accessible how will that effect modern kids and their sexual practices? With such easy communication will we digress or progress in the way we form habits? People get stuck to social media like addictions to heroin. According to online news polls from the telegraph, "social media swallows more than a quarter of time spent online" (Davidson, 2015) "which represents one hour and forty-five minutes a day." And that is only "twenty eight percent of the time the average person spends on the internet." (Davidson, 2015) Meaning people spend on average around four hours a day online. Assuming they sleep on average of eight hours a day, that represents thirty-one percent of their awake time on the internet.

It is safe to say that technology has greatly influenced our habits. However, we should stop and ask ourselves how much of this influence is healthy. Do we want to spend so much of our time invested in social media? We will find out as we move forward into the future that awaits us. As we move forward, we want to think about how the incorporation of technology into society affects our evolution. Will the violence we are exposed to change the way we think? We see clear evidence that soldiers exposed to such horrors of mechanized warfare develop PTSD, but will it affect physical evolution of our brains? From my perspective, any human born of a soldier who developed PTSD will likely have some sort of physical genetic mutation, however minor it may be, in one generation.

It is said that in ancient times, humans had more brain power to remember things and visualize because it was necessary. The Greeks invented countless memory techniques. (Devlin, 2017) Today most hardly memorize each other's phone numbers. Have these progressions of technology worked against the evolution of our brains or simply shifted in a new direction? What will the long term effects of the internet and time spent on there be to the future evolution of our brains. Could we become wired with an ingrained desire for instant gratification and suffer from low attention spans? This should be highly considered if we want the best out of evolution.

Technologies can define a person. Our habits are formed by our surroundings which are now mainly machines, but we should give meaning to the machines and not vice versa. But this concept can be easily overlooked as we give in to what is most comfortable in a life where surviving without hard labor may not be as unconceivable as it once was. Necessities have changed considerably. The rational-mindedness of most scientists has led the way for significant changes in conscious awareness around the world. It is now more than ever that people are aware of the problems and issues facing our society. This global village that Marshall McLuhan coined has brought perceptions closer and closer together. People can now find things to relate with each other easier than ever before representing more points toward breaking away from separation and forming a Global Union led by automation and human ingenuity.

7.3 MEDIA TECHNOLOGY

When war is declared media gets hit first, because it has the power to group people together. Propaganda and the control of knowledge is crucial when you want to control nations. Is media then not a form of mind control? We saw the travesties it created when in the hands of Nazi Germany. Media run by private corporations represents numerous moral hazards that society likely should consider. Everything that goes through the media is filtered by bias opinion of profit seeking representatives. We see the ties with you break open the links between publicly traded conglomerates.

7.3.1   News Broadcasting

News media's influence on elections is considerable if not be complete control. Societal structures, political in particular, were not developed with today's media technologies in mind; those who contributed could never have conceived of future technologies. Yet, we un-notedly follow social technologies without many adjustments; purposed for restoring relativism to new generational advances. Media would best serve society, were it without bias but how can this be accomplished? Well, I'd suggest categorizing, news dissemination, an essential in my needs-based money supply system.

What does this mean for media? Will current companies be placed out of business? No, instead they would simply benefit from money supply to pay their expenses, which would keep objective companies in business, given they have a provable audience. Expenses on their income statements would be brought into existence on occurrence basis. These companies would not be privately owned. Instead, they would be run by the best people for the job all of whose salaries would be guaranteed given they have a provable audience. Incentive structures would be created for companies serving the biggest audiences; therefore, keeping a healthy competitive structure designed to nurture human ingenuity and the best results. This of course comes in due time according to anti-inflation measures.

Approved Media outlets would have their expense accounts funded by the issuing body for money supply. This would alleviate news firms from monetary pressures of business and allow them to focus on reporting objective and relevant news for the Global Union. Journalists would be free to pursue any stories they desire within budget. This does not mean that non-essential media categories could not exist. However, privately held media outlets running under the non-essentials markets would be subject to the rules and regulations of the non-essential market, which should thrive as money supply will be set at an appropriate conversion rate which would ultimately self-adjust according to anti-inflation requirements. Likely requires a complex algorithm for which I do not have the mathematical or programming expertise to develop.

7.3.2   Film and Television

Television and Film are great tools available to the people but act as a double-edged sword. It is clear that certain shows and movies, have strong bias and political motives; regardless if fiction or not. Audiences love to learn from film and television because it shows other's experiences as fun learning opportunities. This is often used to the learning benefit of society, which has been a noble use of fiction. A lot of professional shows teach basic jargon to audiences. Things like Gray's Anatomy or Suits, any show about a profession depicting work environments slightly teaches audiences.

Fiction influences human psychology. Let's not forget what the bible is, a sort of moralized fiction stories that developed much of our historical progress no matter how brutal it may have been. Yet, throughout history we have learned much from it. In regards to category, I would classify entertainment as a non-essential industry. However, documentary or certain heavily teaching orientated shows could be classified as an essentials-service for funding if novel benefit is clearly established. Something like the national film board, hey what do you know, one exists. Professional advisors would approve or deny submitted projects of for essentials classification. Anything that passes must provide a defined benefit for humanity. Money would simply be created to fund the proposed financial budgets for the project which must be reviewed and approved.

7.4 Conclusions

Machines and technological progress have benefited society throughout history; by providing for our survival and comfort. Technology has proved consistently through time that it's our best source of survival and we should collectively view it as so. However, it comes with consequences and obstacles that require attention before we reach the final stage of a world without suffering. I reiterate Nikola Tesla's ideas of wireless energy. I'm not a scientist nor do I have expertise in this field, so please do not hold me to such standards. From my laymen's research on Tesla, it was suppression of technology to serve wealth holding ego's. It seems that for the best overall benefit to society, we should not put up barriers to progress such as patent suppression on essentials inventions. All essentials-based patents would be classified as public domain to be used for the good of the species. Use of them in the luxuries markets would have a reasonable fee that would be an anti-inflation measure. Profiteering and the pursuit of money accumulation can result in inefficient technology. I am not saying there are no patents. Patents deemed non-essentials will hold up as they do now. Those who develop new or improve previous patents in essentials products will hold royalty rights from the money supply system given the patent is in use. Any essentials-based technology should have the incentive for innovation given a benefit to the society.

Again, the benefits should be clearly demonstrated. We have clearly advanced technology to do wonderful things for our industrious expansion and production. But now that water and resource will become more and more of an issue, we must prioritize our needs. By installing a needs-based money supply system, our essentials-based industries are protected from the self-interested agendas that prevent society to operate efficiently. This will protect the interest of the species. Luxuries technology companies would operate in the same manner they do today.

7.4.1   War Driven Technology

Looking at history it is not difficult to notice that throughout time, there have been many empires, great and small which have risen and fallen. This shows us that past attitudes and behaviors did not work. Time and time again we noticed that history's empirical wars led to suffering and enslaving of innocent people. The greatest loss to the species occurred when Archimedes was killed by Roman soldiers during the Second Punic War, because he would not stop working on his mathematical diagrams. He was on the verge of making discoveries that may have gotten us to today's point technologically earlier by hundreds of years. Egos, arrogance, and war are detriments to the species. We are now very late to the plate, and we allowed greed and self-serving egos run society into contrived contextual paradigms.

Our most modern technologies were derivatives of two world wars. Something such as the atom bomb. An invention that should have been left as a blueprint concept, without tests done that permanently morph the earth's natural environment or the internet, which was a military project. Mostly every technology has occurred for reason or another because of war. From Archery to gunpowder to the modern assault rifle, what will be next? What is the use of all these arms? Self-defense. Well to be honest there is no problem with their conceptualizations or production. In fact, considering the infinitely vast number of possibilities of external dangers that may exist outside of our solar system, I do consider weaponry and self-defense technologies a necessity. I am however pro-peace within humanity. Why destroy each other when the forces of nature are what we should be worried about. I also believe that the weapons of today likely should be highly unsophisticated, because it is all terrestrial-based technology that is meant to destroy human beings in our gravitation zone. If we want to protect ourselves from the external natural forces and any possible threatening intelligent forces that may exist in space, we need to think bigger, but first we need an efficient, solid foundation of societal structures that creates a paradigm that will open our minds to this.

After Hiroshima, a cold war, and multiple resource control wars in the middle east have driven machines and technology exceptionally further. Again, terrestrial based drones and automation were applied to extinguish our own kind. It is unlikely that these weapons would have significant effect on anything non-human or non-human technologies. Thus, what is its purpose and utility for the race really? Should we really be playing with guns when we haven't got our collective moralities in check? What seems to be the take away is that we should realize that war has served as a driver of scientific innovation, but we need to harness that competitive spirit into something productive.

7.4.2   Robotics

I do not see the need to infuse robots with strong AI. If Hollywood producers and writers can make the realization in shows like Westworld that we should never give robots complete AI, then scientists do as well. Imagine a world where no human did laborious work, which does not mean zero exercise. We should be deeply involved in our health. However, robotics is the most efficient way to do things. Robotics being a threat to humanity becomes an essential need for the society. Not only for safety for use. All companies working on new developments would have an unlimited amount of capital to work with given they can prove the utility.

The human need being to completely eliminate the need for human beasts of burden in tedious jobs. Thus, if a person can prove their idea will help society get to the point where no one has to suffer as a beast of burden, their budgets will be granted. This would also apply to new improvements on previous automation technologies. Inventors will get a set royalty fee from the money supply authorities, based on the demand or usage of their invention. Everyone involved in bringing the project to life will earn a proportional royalty to their input.

This system would protect society's needs to have security. Luxuries are also important but we should prioritize for survival in the long run. Again, why would we not want robotics doing everything for us while we can proactively enhance evolution through intellectual pursuits and exercise while living in peace? We are not beasts of burden, we are human beings, and we are blessed to be here. So, let's go the distance and make the best of what is available to us. The more we advance the more we will have for everyone, but we should develop robotics and full automation as a human need, but not merge robotics with advanced AI. This is crucial to our survival. If Hollywood can predict it, so can science.

7.4.3   Artificial Intelligence

I don't see a problem with AI, being it is maintained in an isolated network. What's the point of creating an aware AI? You can create an aware human being. AI should be merely a computational tool to serve humanity in making complex computations that are too inefficient for us. For example, creating a computer program that has all the laws of physics programed into it, then program a version of excel's solver to have the AI program spit out blue prints for efficient aerodynamics and space travel engineering machines. It could be used to develop manufacturing automation systems and any other engineering marvel from weapons to toilets. You could insert any result you want and ask the AI for the best design taking into consideration the laws of physics and aerodynamics. This could also be done with biology and could solve molecular biology problems like cancer, and anti-aging. I'm not a programmer but if they can make Solver on excel they could make any of these. This is the sort of AI we want. A sort of solver like in excel but for everything from health to engineering.

We should find a way to create this solver program, because it would be able to give us any invention we desire. Imagine a solver for chemistry and you ask it for all the possible combinations of beneficial chemical combinations to the human genome. This kind of program could give us all the necessary functions and solutions for the most efficient chemical combinations within the body. I am not an expert in this field nor a trained engineer or scientist, I merely feel this would be the best use of AI for society.

7.4.4   Automation

Automation is key to the needs-based money supply system. Society should stop reforming to past political and economic traditions. By classifying automation, a public need in the needs-based-money supply system, we will be prioritizing and accelerating the adoption of such technologies. This will destroy jobs and create unemployment. However, this is what we want in a needs-based-money supply system, because food production, health, and housing would eventually be provided to all citizens of the Global Union by money supply. The new needs markets would encourage these workers to return to school and pursue a passion or simply search out employment in the job markets.

To successfully make the transition, we need to switch to the needs-based-money supply system with as many national letters of intent to join as possible. Only then can we fully implement our automated systems in every aspect of life, and not worry about unemployment. Things like self-driving trucks will put millions out of work. These people need a needs-based-money supply system that will provide for a smooth transition into our next phase of development. Society will be a place where humans simply develop their brains with evolution and are free to pursue their passions as they please. True Freedom can only be accomplished with total automation.

7.4.4.1 *Garbage systems*

The systems currently in place for garbage disposal are immoral and anti-progressive for the species. Why do we still produce non-degradable packaging that piles up creating cities of garbage where people live in. This is from the rapid growth of mass production and consumerism. A more ethical system is one that uses 100% biodegradable materials for the packaging. We need to apply rationality this to all aspects of government and the usage of earth's scarce resource and sustainability.

Imagine a garbage disposal system that works like plumbing and drainage systems. For this to occur, there would need to be regulation that forced all packaging manufacturing to create things that are environmentally friendly and biodegradable. If this can be done, a large dispenser type disposal system could be implemented. These large disposal bins would be placed outside any building and could likely be designed to reach the inside of a person's home or apartment. It would crush and cut the biodegradable packaging into pieces that gets air vacuumed through air tight pipes to the local facility that is in charge of the next process of recycling. This would eliminate the needs of garbage unions and workers. This is a type of automation that has to be an essential system of automation; with the main goal of eliminating human beasts of burden.

7.4.5   Space

The final frontier is where humanity must aim. A google search for how long earth can sustain life will spit out 1.75 billion years given perfect conditions without natural disasters. Astronomical forces will eventually render the planet uninhabitable.

"Somewhere between 1.75 billion and 3.25 billion years from now, Earth will travel out of the solar system's habitable zone and into the "hot zone," new research indicates." (Parry, 2013)

Bewildering how long it took for us to get here in terms of evolution. Because the current form of humans has only been around for the last 200,000 years.

"They calculated that Earth's habitable-zone lifetime is as long as 7.79 billion years. (Earth is estimated to be about 4.5 billion years old.) Meanwhile, the other planets had habitable-zone lifetimes ranging from 1 billion years to 54.72 billion years.

"If we ever needed to move to another planet, Mars is probably our best bet," Rushby said in a statement. "It's very close and will remain in the habitable zone until the end of the sun's lifetime — 6 billion years from now."" (Parry, 2013)

The fact is that if we survive long enough, we need to relocate planets. Sure, we may consider the need for it to be far in the future, however I argue that with the nature of uncertainty no precautions should be underestimated if we want to last. It is not inconceivable that a similar race to our own could have existed on earth in the distant past, say 100,000+ years or 200,000+ years ago. Though, such ideas are nearly impossible to prove and may be unlikely.

7.4.5.1 Aliens

I want to touch on this subject just because it is such an exciting and fun topic to talk about. Do I believe in extra-terrestrial intelligence? I hold it highly probable. Do I believe they have visited earth? Improbable, though not containing a near zero probability. If there is intelligent life out there and they reached the high technological points that scientists on earth can conceive of, then it likely they know about us. Again, with a subject that has not been proved with enough public evidence, we should always hold a very high level of skepticism. However, being that humanity is so vastly different than other creatures of earth, I find the extent of the deviation likely un-coincidental. This could mean nothing, so I will hold reservations on the subject matter at unknown probabilities until solid evidence is discovered shown to me.

To me logically there is a much higher probability of intelligent life existing, because we already know that it does here, which automatically increases the likelihood. The outcome of zero intelligent life is impossible because *we* exist. The outcome of no other intelligent life is only one possible alternative other than the universe having one, being us. One other intelligent species out there is another alternative. The number of alternatives involving more intelligent species existing ranges into literally an infinite number of possibilities. Demonstration of this being that only one other intelligent race exists out there, or two, or three, and so on forever. Therefore, the probability of there being more intelligent life out there infinitely exceeds the one possible alternative of no other intelligent life existing other than us.

This means the probability of no other intelligent life is 1 divided by an infinite number of alternate possibilities all of which contain at least one or more intelligent species. So, the probability of more intelligent life when done in aggregate is infinity minus 1 (the possibility of no life) divided by infinity. From a pure mathematical perspective, it would seem infinitely irrational to consider that no other intelligent life exists whatsoever. The rational perspective would be to try to discover where they are.

In my view, the probabilities of extra-terrestrial life highly hinge on whether the universe is infinite or not, and whether this is a simulation or not. I'm sure you can tell where I'm going with this. If the universe is infinite my probabilities would apply. However, in a finite existence, there would only be a finite number of possibilities making an accurate calculation impossible without the exact numbers. If this is a simulation not only would it likely require an intelligent creator, but also, we would have to question the need to create any real space beyond what humanity can reach. Distance could easily be an illusion so strong it fools telescopes. To me, it is all uncertain, and, because of the complexities of what each idea determines these concepts may be illusive to prove. Not only that, we cannot be sure whether physical reality and laws of physics are constant or malleable beyond our existence or within it. To me it would make sense that many different life forms come into existence in different sorts of environments in ways we cannot conceive. Like the entities that live within hot volcanic temperatures.

7.4.5.2 *Problems with assuming no intelligent life.*

In assuming we are the only intelligent life in creation we effectively leave ourselves vulnerable and unprepared for the advent that we are incorrect. From my perspective it is infinitely likely they exist. By assuming we are alone, we will always find ourselves looking to each other as enemies.

7.5 ISSUES

A lot of issues will arise with transition into a money supply system. As we approach full automation, we may have to keep tax in the non-essentials markets as a way to fight inflation. This tax would not be in the form of income but rather only sales tax that should be variable and linked to stable inflation. At first, transition into such a needs-based dollar system may be resisted by those with established long-term plans for the current system. We have to look aside our differences to expand the pie for the species. Everyone comes out a winner in this model.

Natural truth is many things could develop rationales to be defined as essential to the survival but prioritization is key to efficiency for society. Being beasts of burden is no one's desire and by letting a few hands control our essential technologies humanity will likely have a difficult time coming together in a time of catastrophic need. If we can unite and prioritize our survival by classifying all robotics, automation, news media, and education first, we can work up to the rest as we gain experience with a new system.

When something comes along that threatens our survival we can kick its ass because together we can may every likely even be capable of withstanding the longest test of time in the universe with knowledge not yet uncovered. We are the same organism all in one creating ourselves in different versions here on earth. Let's treasure ourselves and our futures. Let's realize that there is a long time left, and likely a shit load of hurdles before the final chapter, so let's get to it, because what I see is a more productive galactic civilization where everyone is enlightened in its original sense of the word. Not one of equality outcome but equality of opportunity. Where no one is left suffering, but to earn luxuries one has to contribute. Do we not want that? Will we continue to think in purely self-interest terms and claim that we create products and services for people's good, but charging the highest plausible profit margins? Not saying there is no space for it, because I love those things, but let's keep it separate from the things that matter most to our survival.

8 COMMON GOAL

The founding fathers had the concepts of morality correct in stating everyone is equal. History shows that regardless of their enlightened awareness of these natural rights and freedoms, the societal structures of their time had not caught up with morality. So, we see a lag between morality and societal structures. A lag that we still feel to this day. There's always a lag between novel ideas and their implementation into practice. Our collective habits seem to consistently slow the process down.

The founding father's idea of a government seemed to be a proponent of morality. What we can easily overlook is that this view applies to all humanity. Uniting the race is the next logical step. Not by force or economically crippling nations. History shows that doesn't work. It was the best thing for the early colonists on the losing end of mercantilism and it's the best thing for the species when it comes to overall longest survival. Hamilton and Jefferson painted a black and white picture of how things should run. Industrialization works, but we need balance as we see that nature also requires balance to sustain a livable environment. For me the most important humanly pursuit is terra forming. We should terra form our own earth to better sustain life. We have our lab right in front of us.

Surprises me to know we have not united as a species. In the 60's, people were all about this idea... being equal. What does equal mean? Not wealth distribution... communism doesn't work. What we have going with capitalism is on the right track, but the complexity of humanity's environment and survival within it are more important than pure capitalism. We may be best benefited by considering the best long-term plan for survival of the species through efficient allocation of resources. While many in power have ways to gain and hold control over each other and our resources, we likely should consider the ultimate long-term survival of as many of us as possible. We likely should re-connect with nature and the natural process of evolution and align our societal structures to compliment this.

Societal structure would best benefit us if they complement nature's natural evolution of biodiversity and self-sustainability while providing us everything we need from it. Furthermore, societal structures largely influence our psychology and behavior. That is not to say that at the individual level there is no benefit for change, but at the individual level, the change will not affect the masses. Moral virtues that everyone understands in theory are tough to accomplish in practice, so a need exists for societal structures to be the pillars of human morality.

8.1 ROOT OF GLOBAL SEPARATION

Many problems around the world seem to root from the debt-based money supply systems that we implement today. The systems results include bad wealth distribution, depression, famines, and global suffering. Fractional reserve banking prints money based on debts, which is a classic servitude structure, which ultimately separates the lender from the borrower. We are people trying to guess our futures without knowing what lies ahead. To secure ourselves from this uncertainty we should unite in order to be most effective against any dangers that may appear. Fractional reserve banking's debt-based dollar creates separation. Separation is a poison for humanity and one of the biggest threats to survival.

8.2 COMMON THREATS

The nuclear clock in the united states sits at the highest position since the 1953. We know that life on earth and likely the universe will seize to exist one day, but for us to survive as long as humanely possible, we should unite the species. Old religion knew that union was good when they saw the catastrophes of natural disasters. Unification has been behind human progress from the very beginning. So why stop now, when we know it to be the most beneficial state for the species? Fighting amongst each other is counterproductive.

8.3 ALL FOR THE SPECIES

I believe crime would mostly disappear provided suffering is taken care of with a needs-based monetary system. Imagine you didn't have to worry about shelter or food, and that it was the species goal to make all physical labor taken care of by automation and technology. Our responsibilities would mainly be to evolve our brains and bodies, have kids if we desired, and then be free to enjoy life. That is a world we can live in. It doesn't take much. We have already achieved so much and laid so much foundation that, we are almost there already. Now what remains is a shift in moral conscious. We need each other and we should unite if we want to achieve our max potential. There is no way we have reached it, nor have conceived of it, but to get closer, we likely should take action. We have much to do, and we can be sure that we are not at our best yet. Time to put aside cultural differences and work together as a unit.

We have a lot going for us, and now is the time to take advantage of this progress. The era for individualistic and monopolistic behaviors over our necessities must come to an end. However, that space will remain open in the luxuries-based industries which will be fueled by the money supply system that keeps secures the needs of global citizens. World peace can only be achieved if everyone has their essential needs taken care of. Anything else would result in separation and lead way to a dog eat dog world. Instead, by building strong minded- self-aware individuals that are conditioned for highly active brains from an early age, we will proactively enhance evolution and avoid many social problems. We are too short run oriented and may be failing to see the bigger picture. Life is precious and when someone sets a rate on what your life is worth, we lose sight of just how precious life really is. We cannot see the future and the past is never all too clear. Like many old clichés; the present is where we should be focused.

We have a common goal of survival. We as a society know that we aren't going to last forever on this planet. That is one of the only guarantees that we have. The inevitable destruction of our planet. People will always laugh and say, well, not in my generation. Doesn't mean we shouldn't be prepared. We like the feeling of being correct, but reality is quite uncertain and the only things we can be sure of are the temporary nature of things in this physical realm. It is naïve to ever think we have reached the best structures for society. Societal structures must be malleable and consistently reanalyzed and improved. I have seen many sides of the world and found that people, no matter where, want to avoid suffering, spend time with loved ones, and find our personal happiness. We all have this in common.

In The Name of Progress: An alternative economic model.

147

9 BIBLIOGRAPHY

Antoine Bechara, A. R. (2002). Insensitivity to future consequences following damage to human prefrontal cortex. Cognition, 7-15.

Davidson, L. (2015, May 17). Is your daily social media usage higher than average? Retrieved April 08, 2018

Devlin, H. (2017, Mar 08). The Guardian. Retrieved April 08, 2018

How Has the Human Brain Evolved? (n.d.). Retrieved from Scientific American: www.scientificamerican.com/article/how-has-human-brain-evolved/

Mellstrom, U. (Autumn 2002). Patriarchal Machines and Masculine Embodiment. Science, Technology, & Human Values, Vol. 27, No. 4, p. 460-478.

Parry, W. (2013, Sept 18). How Much Longer Can Earth Support Life? Retrieved from www.livescience.com: www.livescience.com/39775-how-long-can-earth-support-life.html

The Benefits of Feeling Competitive. (2013, Sept 10). Retrieved from Psychology Today: www.psychologytoday.com/ca/blog/compassion-matters/201309/the-benefits-feeling-competitive

www.ingramcontent.com/pod-product-compliance
Lightning Source LLC
Chambersburg PA
CBHW051305250726
48656CB00004B/1488